Author and creator Annette Sym
Food stylist Bill Sym
Photography by Anthony Michael,
Alison Blake, Sally Haxton
Graphics and layout by Jake Thomas
Dietitian tips by Lisa Cochrane BSc.
Grad Dip Diet. MPH APD

Published in 2008 by
Symply Too Good Pty Ltd.
22 Moorabinda Street,
Buderim Queensland 4556
Australia

www.symplytoogood.com

ISBN: 9780957716179
Printed in the USA.

Information was processed using Food
Works 2007 Version 5 and FoodWorks
Version 9.02. Brands named in this
book are suggestions only. The
owners of such brand names retain
all right, title and interest in any to
their respective brands. Every effort
has been made to ensure that the
information in this book was correct
at the time of printing. However the
author and dietitian shall not accept
responsibility for any inaccuracies.

Cooking spray used in the recipes has
not been calculated into the nutritional
information breakdowns due to the
difficulty of calculating the amounts
used by each individual person.

JAN – 2 2010

W9-BWS-063

Welcome

Welcome to my world of healthy low-fat cooking.

I am very excited that you have my first edition of SYMPLY TOO GOOD TO BE TRUE the American Version. I believe I can offer a solution to anyone who has struggled with their weight. For those who are not confident in the kitchen and for those who want to provide healthy meals for their family then this cookbook is for you.

For many years of my life I battled an addiction: FOOD. Food was my greatest weakness but I was able to turn this weakness into my greatest strength, and now you can learn the tools that I taught myself to win the battle of the bulge. I didn't lose 70lbs and maintain this weight to this day just by luck. I had a strategy, a plan and goals that I worked towards so through my tips and recipes I hope you too can become the healthy person you deserve to be.

I know that I used to be an emotional eater. When I was happy I ate, when I was sad I ate and when I was lonely, bored, tired you name it...I ate. What chance did I have with this type of attitude? No wonder I was constantly battling obesity from an early age. All my life I felt like I was different. Kids can be so cruel, and with my nickname of PORKY it wasn't any wonder I turned to food for comfort.

I had a difficult childhood, which led me to think of food as my friend, but it turned into my enemy. All I ask is for you to be open to change, to look at what you have been doing up until today that hasn't been working for you. Just because you have cooked a certain way all your life doesn't mean that it's the right way. I will show you the simplest, most easiest way to cook your favourite recipes, and when you know you can have a piece of cheesecake, a serve of fries, or tacos that are both healthy and taste delicious you will find the inner strength to step up and make the changes necessary to your diet and lifestyle.

I'm not asking you to do anything that I haven't already done myself. I sometimes wonder what my life would be like if I hadn't lost weight all those years ago, but I don't think it would be a pretty picture, so don't wait another minute - get cooking and don't forget my 28 Day Weight Loss Plan. This is ideal for those who need guidance and portion control.

In my book you have the tools that may help you achieve many things, such as:
1) Providing healthy meals for the family that are deliciously guilt-free
2) Recipes that are recommended for anyone who wants to have a healthy diet
3) Recipes that are so healthy they are suitable for people with diabetes.
4) Never feel deprived again. Yes you can have your cake and eat it too, just do it my way.
5) A great way to help save money. Junk food and takeouts are costly. There is nothing better than a home cooked meal so enjoy my easy, quick and tasty recipes and watch those pounds fall away.

Be empowered to make the changes you need to make right now, this very minute. The moment you take responsibility for yourself and your actions is the moment that you can achieve what your heart desires - good health and happiness. I know first hand how hard it is to be overweight, and dieting only makes you fat. The first three letters of the word diet are, die, so that sums it up well. Forget dieting and instead become a healthy person. I'm not asking you to do anything that I haven't already done myself so good luck. I know you can do it.

Happy cooking ♡ Annette

Keeping Motivated

Most people who struggle with their weight will say that lack of motivation and commitment cause them to fail on any diet or health program long term. If you can relate to yo-yo dieting, binge eating and feelings of being out of control then get excited because I have created something that may help you. I believe that being committed to your weight loss journey and feeling empowered to be the best you can be are vital if you wish to lose weight and keep it off forever.

I know from my own personal experience how challenging losing weight can be, but I also know the rewards that await you when you succeed. I have been at my goal range now for many years but I still remember how it feels to battle with your weight, which is why I have put together my 28 Day Weight Loss Plan and included it in this cookbook. I know it will help those who struggle to stay on a diet. Eating a balanced diet and exercising are the keys to weight loss success, but if you are not motivated nothing will work. You must change the habits that caused you to be overweight in the first place so here are some tips to help keep you motivated:

1. Take responsibility for yourself and your actions. Make sure you have food in the house that you can eat that won't cause you problems e.g. if you're not in control of chocolate. Don't have any in your house, car or workplace.

2. Don't be boring with your food, as this will weaken your motivation and commitment.

3. Focus on what you want to achieve, not what you are missing out on. For example, think about how fabulous you will look in those small size jeans or how good it will feel to be able to wear a belt. Imagine how much energy you will have once you lose those pounds and how good you will feel about yourself. Forget about feeling sorry for yourself and only allow positive thoughts to own you.

4. Take each day as it comes and make today the best it can be. Get excited, the new slim you will be here soon - all you have to do is keep motivated and committed to the job at hand.

5. Reward yourself along the way. Acknowledge and celebrate every 10lbs. I did something nice for myself such as having a facial, buying a book or going to the movies.

6. Put positive quotes all over the house, especially in the kitchen.

7. Find a fabulous photo that you love of yourself when you were slim and put it on the refrigerator or somewhere you can look at it a lot.

8. Say I can, I must and I will. Positive self talk is important to long-term success.

9. Focus on what you want to achieve and let nothing stand in your way. You may fall down but so what, pick yourself up, dust yourself off and begin again. Success is your only option.

10. Finally, give yourself a pat on the back every time you do something good and be proud of what you are doing to make your life the best it can be. Love yourself for who you are no matter what shape or size you are.

Annette's Story

As I reflect back over my life, memories as a chubby child, cuddly teenager, buxom bride and an obese adult come to mind. This is the story of how I was able to turn my greatest weakness, food, into my greatest strength. I once weighed 220lbs, but after 20 months of being a healthy person I successfully lost 70lbs, reaching my goal weight in 1993 and have maintained my weight ever since. My journey has been filled with many highs and lows battling years of obesity, but losing weight truly changed my life. Let's go back to where it all began...

A CHUBBY CHILD

Being the fattest kid in my class was something that I got used to. Everyone told me (and my mother) that it was "baby fat" and I would lose it, so I lived in ignorant bliss and just waited for the day that it would all melt away. That day never came. Life continued where I had to buy my clothes from the women's section, as the children's section could not cater to size. Being overweight as a kid wasn't easy, so I made up for it by being happy and outgoing, all the time desperate to fit in, yet crying on the inside. My way of surviving was to laugh at myself and dream of the day that I would look like all the other girls. I just wanted to be normal.

CUDDLY TEENAGER

At the age of 13 I weighed 183lbs and discovered dieting. A doctor gave me diet pills and boy did I lose weight. When I think back I am horrified at what my eating pattern was like - I would eat nothing until lunchtime and then only either an apple or a yogurt. Dinner was a piece of steak, a little mashed potato and peas. Yes, the weight did fall off me but as you would expect I couldn't sustain this restricted diet, and too soon I was back eating the wrong foods and the weight came back with a vengeance. Teenagers can be so cruel, and nicknames cut deep. My nickname at high school was "Porky".

BUXOM BRIDE

I was married at 19 to the man of my dreams. I had to have my wedding dress made as I weighed around 176lbs. After two years of contented, blissful marriage my weight blew up to 210lb. I was getting fatter by the minute. I remember one time I was in a shop and the man behind the counter asked me when was I due to give birth. I mumbled some sort of response and just ran home sobbing my fat little heart out. The funny thing is that you would think that would make me lose weight but all it did was turn me more to my old friend food for comfort.

OBESE ADULT

This is where my true addiction to food really took over. Food was my best friend: it didn't judge me and was always there for me. I was always on some sort of diet, searching for the easy way to lose weight. Crazy diets that involved starving, liquid only diets, pills, hypnosis, pre-packaged meals, every diet book and magazine that I could find, and let's not forget the cabbage soup diet – that was a real doozy. All these diets achieved in the end was weight gain and money wasted. Having three children only made the battle harder but occasionally I did have successes. Looking through my photo albums, some years weren't too bad, but eventually I would re-gain my weight, and more. Then one day I had a life changing experience when my best friend Kim took a photo of me at the beach (January 1992). I weighed 220lbs and was feeling very self-conscious. Two weeks later she sent me the photo - it was like a slap across the face. I cried the whole day: I had reached as low as I could go. But as I wiped away the tears, something happened, I stopped feeling sorry for myself and decided that I had to do something about it. I stopped dieting and the rest is history. I not only conquered my weight problem but also created a life filled with an abundance of happiness. I turned my greatest weakness into my greatest strength.

HEALTHY PERSON

The day I stopped dieting is the day I won my battle of the bulge. Learning to cook my favorite meals the low-fat way, getting active and embracing the concept of being a healthy person changed my life and I know if you can relate to my story then you too can change your life. My story is about being addicted to food and turning my life around to become a person who is now healthy and eating delicious food. My story is about daring to dream, embracing that dream and running with it. Don't wait another minute, empower yourself to be the best you can be and believe that it will happen. Don't let anything stand in your way and don't believe for another moment that you don't deserve to wear the clothes you want to, to feel good about yourself and love yourself. Don't wait for a slap across the face situation like I did - start now and change your life. All it takes is for you to make the decision like I did to become a healthy person and reap the rewards. Be your own best friend, not your worst enemy. Talk to yourself in a loving way and forget all the past failures. Start with a fresh, new attitude and remember,
if I did it so can you.

♡ Annette

Annette's Tips

1. **Read the labels on products.** "Light" doesn't always mean "low-fat". For example, light olive oil only means it is light in color or flavour. Light could also mean that it is light in quantity, salt, sugar, fat or texture. Look for products that are both low in fat and sugar. Cholesterol-free means the product is low in saturated fats, but could still be a high-fat product as they use vegetable oil instead of animal fat. This is ideal for someone watching their cholesterol but not so good for a slimmer.

2. **Go for reduced-fat dairy products** such as low-fat milk, yogurt, cheese and dips. Forget full-fat milk at nearly 10g of fat compared to the best choice - no-fat milk. Avoid using cream and instead use low-fat 2% evaporated milk and instead of butter use low-fat margarine

3. **Always eat breakfast**, it kicks-starts your metabolism for the day.

4. **Drink at least 8 glasses** (4 pints) of water every day. Dehydration can be mistaken for hunger and drinking adequate amounts of water really helps the body deal with fluid retention and getting rid of waste products.

5. **Cut down on caffeine**; I suggest you convert to de-caffeinated versions instead. A low-sodium diet is beneficial, as we generally consume far too much salt. By limiting the amount of salt in your diet you can reduce fluid retention and also help lower blood pressure.

6. **Junk food can be high in fat**, high in sugar and high in salt with very little fiber and therefore is best eaten only occasionally not daily. Always eat breakfast, it kicks-starts your metabolism for the day.

7. Have **alcohol in moderation** too much and healthy eating goes out the window. Alcohol is high in sugar and if consumed too often, can cause weight gain.

8. Eat the **quantities of food** that your body needs. When serving your meal always use the sizing guide of a quarter protein, a quarter carbohydrates and half the plate filled with vegetables or salad. Think about how much your body needs, not what you want. You can never eat too many vegetables or salad, but too many carbohydrates or proteins can cause weight gain. Everything in moderation is the key to portion sizing.

9. **Take control of food**, do not allow food to control you.

10. **Think and act** like a healthy person.

11. **Exercise** 5-6 times a week.

12. **Don't be a chronic dieter** instead come into my world and enjoy low-fat food the way it should be. Be satisfied, full and not deprived. Be happy, think positive and live life to the fullest every day. I know you can do it!

10 TIPS TO LOW-FAT COOKING

- Use cooking sprays instead of adding oil or fats to the pan.

- Buy lean meats. For example, 4% ground beef is so much lower in fat and much better than normal ground beef. The difference is that when the butcher makes the ground beef he puts more fat in the machine. Buy lean meat and you will be leaner.

- Remove the skin off the chicken or turkey or better still buy without the skin. The thigh is also higher in fat, so choose the breast as it is the leanest part.

- Forget deep-frying - grill, barbeque or bake instead using cooking spray or baking paper.

- Make coconut cream my way – low-fat 2% evaporated milk and a little coconut extract.

- Use low-fat mayonnaise and no-oil dressing on your salads.

- Choose only reduced-fat margarines and no-fat milk for your baking.

- In most of my baking I tend to throw out egg yolks. Why? Well the yolk has 6g of fat and is high in saturated fats. The egg white has all the nutrients and raising ability but has no fat, so why put yolks in if they don't benefit the dish.

- In some of my baking I like to use apple sauce (in jar) instead of oil or butter in cakes/muffins. Apple sauce gives the moisture butter would normally give, but there is no fat in apples.

- I then add baking soda to the apple sauce as it will help keep cakes or muffins lighter.

Liquid Measures

Metric	Imperial
5ml (1 teaspoon)	⅛fl oz
10ml (1 dessertspoon)	⅓fl oz
15ml (1 tablespoon)	½fl oz
30ml	1fl oz
125ml	4fl oz
150ml	5fl oz (¼ pint)
250ml	8fl oz
300ml	10fl oz (½ pint)
500ml	16fl oz
600ml	20fl oz (1 pint)
1000ml (1 liter)	32fl oz (1¾ pints)

Dry Measures

Metric	Imperial
15g	½oz
30g	1oz
114g	4oz(¼lb)
227g	8oz (½lb)
340g	12oz (¾lb)
454g	16oz (1lb)
680g	24oz(1½lb)
908g	32oz (2lbs)

Oven Temperatures

Keep in mind the temperatures will vary between different types, brands and size of the oven. Different manufacturers and oven types do vary, so always refer to your cooker instruction book.

IF YOU DON'T HAVE A FAN FORCED OVEN

As a general rule if you don't have a fan-forced oven then you should set your temperatures 10-20 degrees higher than what is called for in the recipe. Cooking times will also be longer so add around 10 minutes more for every hour of cooking time in the recipes.

	C°(Celsius)	F°(Fahrenheit)	Gas Mark
Slow	275	140	1
Slow	300	150	2
Moderate	325	170	3
Moderate	350	180	4
Moderate hot	375	190	5
Moderate hot	400	200	6
Hot	425	220	7
Hot	450	230	8
Very hot	475	240	9

Portion Distortion

Have you checked the size of dinner plates lately? Our meal portions at home and eating out are getting larger and it shows as we are getting larger as well. I remember when I was a kid our plates, dessert bowls and drinking glasses were so much smaller than they are today. This could explain why we are now bigger than ever before in history. Adding to the problem is the time we are spending sitting on the couch and not exercising. Here are some tips to help you understand what normal portion sizes are.

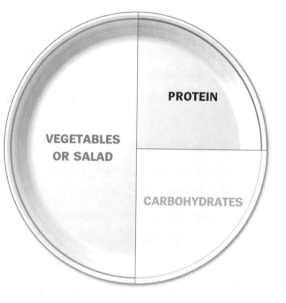

1. The size of meat you should have at dinner time should be about the size of the palm of your hand - 3oz for women and 4oz for men is a good portion for weight loss.

2. Rice (cooked) should be between ½ to ¾ of a cup for women and 1 cup for men.

3. Spaghetti noodles (cooked) should be 1 cup for women and 1½ for men.

4. Women should have no more than 2-3 average serves of fruit a day and men should have 3-4 serves. An average serve should weigh about 5oz.

5. Vegetables are unlimited but this does not include potato, corn, peas or avocado. These choices need to be portion controlled.

6. Counting calories is important, for example you could be eating low-fat crackers but a huge amount of calories. Check the labels of products.

7. Weigh your food for a few days to see how much you are having. You might be surprised. For example I asked my husband how much cereal he ate in the morning. He weighed it and was shocked to find out he was eating double what he really should be having. Ignorance is not bliss and can be the reason why you may have struggled to lose weight.

8. Soda pops are way over consumed. There are around 28 teaspoons in a 34fl oz bottle of soda pop and around 10 teaspoons in a can so loads of calories here. I would suggest you avoid sugary drinks such as sodas, energy drinks and juices.

9. Don't eat on the run. It is much better to sit and take your time - savor your moment.

10. Most times we confuse thirst with being hungry, so drink lots of water and see if this helps keep your hunger at bay.

11. Don't eat just for the sake of it, out of habit or from boredom. Next time you eat something ask yourself are you eating because the clock says it's time to eat or because you are actually hungry?

12. Just because you think certain foods are healthy doesn't mean you can over eat it, such as nuts, avocado and fruit. Everything needs to be eaten in moderation for weight loss success.

13. Packets of potato chips and snacks have grown larger. Don't sit down to watch TV with a 10oz pack of chips. It is so easy to just eat the contents without even being aware of what you are doing. Instead measure out no more than 2oz in a bowl.

14. Try not to have takeaways and drive-through meals as a regular part of your week and don't fall into the trap of upsizing just because it's only 50 cents extra. Think about what the cost to your health and your weight will be.

15. Never go back for seconds.

Tips When Dining Out

We all love to go out and enjoy a meal at a restaurant, but when you are trying to lose weight it can be a nightmare. Choosing from a huge menu can be intimidating and confusing, so here are some tips:

• Ideal choices are seafood but keep it as natural as possible. Grilled, instead of fried, is a great way to have fish.

• Avoid anything that is deep fried, battered or crumbed.

• Normally restaurant meals are large so have an appetizer and then choose another appetizer for your entrée. I always order a side of either vegetables or salad as well.

• Forget the high fat garlic or herb bread. If you must have bread then instead ask for fresh crusty bread rolls.

• Cream-based sauces are out. Instead order the tomato-based dishes which are much lower in fat.

• Don't arrive at the restaurant starving as you will order up everything and eat everything in sight. Have a piece of fruit, or something to take the edge off your hunger before you leave the house.

• Drink lots of water before you arrive at the restaurant so you don't arrive thirsty. Once there start with water or soda pop then as the meal progresses have a glass of wine but mix it with soda water or orange juice and mix spirits with diet soda pop. Alcohol has loads of calories so go back to drinking water as soon as possible.

• Often chefs will drown the meat or chicken in sauce so ask for the sauce to be served on the side. Same with salad dressing - have it served separately so you control how much you have.

• Any soup starting with the word CREAMY will more than likely be based on cream. Better choices would be clear soups or soups that are based on vegetables such as minestrone.

• If you love to have a dessert follow these tips
(1) share with your partner or friend - this way you only have a small serving which most times is all you need and you leave feeling satisfied.
(2) Order a fresh seasonal fruit plate.
(3) Instead of ordering dessert order a low-fat cappuccino - you most probably will find this will satisfy your sweet tooth enough and you won't need a dessert at all.

If you do overeat then compensate the next day by having a lighter day with your food choices or increase your exercise for a couple of days to help compensate. Remember dining out is not just about food, it is about having a great time with good company so make wise choices and take your good intentions with you. I guarantee you'll be glad you did.

Get Active

It is a proven fact that being active and eating a balanced amount of fat and calories are the keys to weight loss success. Most people can't manage their weight successfully unless they combine good nutrition and regular exercise. Physical activity combined with healthy eating habits help achieve the right balance to good health and wellbeing. Exercise also relieves stress as it releases endorphins that give you a rush of energy and vitality, so grab your runners and get moving.

Here are some tips to get you started:

- Schedule time in your day for exercise, otherwise it just won't happen.

- Do lots of different types of exercise, that way you won't get bored.

- If you are unfit start exercising slowly and work your way up. Too much too soon can cause strains and damage to muscles and ligaments.

- Ask a friend to walk or exercise with you. This may help keep your commitment strong.

- Get a good pair of runners that have arch support.

- Walking is an easy way to get fit. Increase your challenges by walking up hills or on the beach, or do bursts of skipping and running.

- Exercising will help reduce stress and tension levels.

- Park your car at a distance from the shops and take the stairs instead of the elevator. All these 5-10 minute walks really do add up and help burn fat.

- Join a gym or fitness centre. Especially in winter this is a good option.

- Yoga is a fantastic way to get fit and help stress management.

- For weight loss exercise 5-6 times a week. Exercising 3 times a week will help maintain weight. A great way to support weight loss is to be as active as possible.

- Middle age spread has little to do with getting older. Too little exercise is the main culprit.

- The best type of exercise is one that you are able to sustain comfortably for at least 30 minutes.

- The best thing to do when you are tired is to exercise, which not only picks you up but also will make you feel better.

- You will have a longer and better quality of life if you get active. It's never too late, so start now.

Glycemic Index

Most foods that we eat are made up of a mix of the three main nutrients: carbohydrate, fat, and protein. Carbohydrate foods are one of the best sources of energy for our body, being the preferred fuel for our muscles and most of our organs. Foods high in carbohydrate include fruit, milk, yogurt, breads, cereals, legumes (e.g. beans, lentils, chickpeas) and starchy vegetables like corn, potato and sweet potato.

Of course, not all carbohydrate foods are the same: nearly all are digested and converted to glucose, but they do so at different rates – some slow, some fast. Once upon a time, carbohydrate foods were grouped according to how much sugar and starch (complex carbohydrate) they contained. Foods high in simple sugars include fruit, dairy foods, and table sugar, whereas foods high in starch include breads, cereal, legumes, and starchy vegetables. This system of classifying carbohydrates was based on the physical structure of the carbohydrate in the food. It was assumed that simple sugars were quickly absorbed into the blood while starches were slowly absorbed. Based on these assumptions, people were advised to eat mainly starches and to limit foods that were high in simple sugars.

In the 1980's, a new method of classifying carbohydrate foods, called the Glycemic Index, was developed. It proved once and for all that all sugars are not absorbed quickly into the blood and that not all starches are slowly absorbed.

So what is Glycemic Index or GI? The GI is a ranking of carbohydrates in food according to their effect on blood glucose (sugar) levels after eating. Foods with a low GI (55 or less) cause blood glucose level to rise more slowly over a longer period of time than high GI foods (70 or more). So low-GI foods are the best choices when trying to maintain constant energy levels, and when aiming to keep blood glucose levels lower for longer. High-GI foods, on the other hand, are useful during prolonged physical activity (longer than one hour) or for treating hypoglycemia.

Not all carbohydrate foods eaten need to be low-GI, however. Authorities recommend that you try to eat at least one serve of low-GI carbohydrates at each meal, or base at least two meals each day on low-GI choices. The table lists commonly eaten lower-GI foods:

Recipes in this book have the Glycemic Index ranked as either low, medium or high which I have calculated for Annette to help you maintain optimal energy and blood glucose levels.

Dr Alan Barclay
B Sc: Grad Dip; PhD

Food Groups	Examples
Breads	Wholegrain, multigrain, fruit loaf
Cereals	Pasta, noodles, etc... Basmati or Doongara rice, breakfast cereals e.g. All-bran, Guardian, Komplete, Traditional Rolled Oats, etc...
Vegetables - starchy	Sweet potato, sweet corn
Legumes	All beans (except broad), lentils and chickpeas
Fruits	Orchard fruits: e.g. apple, orange, pear, peach, plum, and grapes.

Success stories

Many wonderful people have written letters, faxes and emails from all over the world. I feel blessed that so many people have taken the time out of their busy lives to write to me and I thank you all. I thought I would share some fantastic snippets from mail that I have received.

Thank you Annette, your books have been my greatest inspiration to losing weight. I have been overweight from the age of 7. Over the years I just gradually got bigger. I had tried every diet and joined almost every club, only ever with short-term success, the diets were always so boring. I lost 88lbs in 18 months and feel truly wonderful. I've never been happier or more confident. I will always use your books Annette and plan on never gaining weight again.

Gail Alford
Moffat Beach, QLD Australia

My cholesterol thanks to medication and your recipes has gone from 10 down to 4.4 in eight weeks. The lowest it has ever been and I am ecstatic.

Ann Menzies
Manoora, QLD Australia

I spent most of my adult life as a morbidly obese person. Until I said enough was enough! I decided to become smart about weight loss. I changed the way I thought and the way I ate and became less than half the person I use to be; losing 170lbs. When losing weight; a person needs to change everything including the way they think.

My book The Thinking Side to Thin shows you how to change the way you think and arms you with information that keeps you on track. Annette's books, shows you how to eat right, in such a way that it becomes a healthy lifestyle instead of a diet. Annette and I met when she was on my radio show Amazing Women, brains, beauty & style. When I received her books with all her great recipes I knew she understood what losing weight was all about; and she truly is an Amazing Woman. Annette is a passionate and smart author, cook and weight-loss guru. Dr Marlene.

Marlene Siersema, Ph.D.
California USA

After visiting your website I quickly ordered your books. I can't begin to tell you what a change your recipes have brought to our lives and just at the right time. My husband has cholesterol and high blood pressure problems and I've been battling a weight problem for years, plus Yo-yo dieting. My husband has lost 18lbs and I've lost 22lbs. We both feel so healthy and wow there's no getting bored with all those recipes. I haven't seen any health recipe books in our bookstores here in South Africa that come anywhere near yours. Yours are beautifully illustrated and having the nutritional break down is so very helpful.

Brenda Greeff
Cape Town, SOUTH AFRICA

I was lucky enough to attend one of your seminars, I say lucky because it changed my life forever. You are such an inspirational speaker and I left that night knowing I was going to lose weight, get healthy and be the person I wanted to be. I proudly tell you that I'm now at my ideal weight, having lost 50lbs and feel fantastic. Using your recipes has taught me so much, thank you.

Tracey Charters
Ipswich, QLD Australia

I am a great believer in your books. I have type 2 diabetes and had to lose weight and was shown your books. I have now gone down 6 dress sizes and have kept my weight down for the past few years and feel great. I had been taking blood pressure tablets for 13 years and now I don't have to, and my diabetes is under control. I hope this letter gives other readers encouragement.

Beaty Sterling
Oonoonba, QLD Australia

We discovered your cookbooks while visiting my sister last year. My sister had been using your recipes and had lost 25lbs and looked great. We even lost weight while we were there as they used your recipes all the time and we both came home five pounds lighter and had eaten really good food! We now have our own copies and so do my two daughters and sister who live in Canada, we all love them.

Jean Dodson
California, U.S.A.

Thank you for your recipe books. I call them my bibles. My whole family loves the recipes, they are nice and easy for me as a busy wife and mother of 4. I have managed to lose 62lbs since cooking with your books.

Wendy Schwanda
Burnie, TAS Australia

Thank you for your wonderful cookbooks. They were recommended to me by the dietitian after my heart by-pass operation. They have become my bibles and go everywhere with me, even when we travel in our caravan.

Tamara Genders
Mountain Creek, QLD Australia

I just want to say thank so much for your cookbooks I absolutely love them. I was introduced to them by my sister who uses them to help with her diabetes. I use your cookbooks daily and have lost over 66lbs.

Karin Griffiths
Rockingham, WA Australia

I have tried various diets with short term success, however the weight loss would always end up coming back. I am pleased to say I have just reached my goal weight thanks to the changes in lifestyle I achieved through better food choices, portion control and thanks to your excellent recipes. It has taken me 12 months to lose 100lbs and I feel sure that I have reformed my bad eating habits so that I can keep the weight off for good. There is no doubt in my mind that your recipe books have improved my lifestyle in such a way to coin a familiar phrase, Its "SYMPLY TOO GOOD TO BE TRUE"

Peter Cathery
Mooroolbark VIC Australia

My husband Lindsay lost 55lbs in just over one year and has kept it off, just by following your wonderful recipes. He says he never feels hungry or deprived and I love it because the whole family are eating meals that are healthy and enjoyable. My job is easy now thanks to your cookbooks.

Jenny and Lindsay Heperi
Christchurch, NEW ZEALAND

Both my husband and myself send you our heartfelt thanks for your fantastic books. We now only use your cookbooks. With your recipes and a little exercise my husband has lost 66lbs and I have lost 68lb. We both feel the fittest and healthiest we have in years.

Sue Kelly
Gaven Heights, QLD Australia

As soon as I started using your books I realised I had been cheating myself. I am no longer deprived any more and enjoy eating healthy, nutritious meals. I now have achieved my goal weight and my health has improved and I have so much more energy. I am so happy and confident compared to the old me that once weighed 286lbs. I now weigh 154lbs – Annette you saved my life.

Cathy Chapman
Reservoir, VICTORIA Australia

Being a long distance truck driver I needed simple recipes that could travel with me in my truck. Your recipes have shown me how to be satisfied and enjoy eating again. I have lost 110lbs and feel the best I have ever felt in my life.

John Moore
Pomona, QLD Australia

I was having chemotherapy for cancer. As I am overweight the doctors told me to go on a diet, but not to expect to lose weight whilst on the program. My sister put me onto your books and I haven't looked back. Even with chemo I have been able to lose 46lbs in 6 months, everyone was amazed. Your recipes are so nice why would anyone want to eat the high fat way? I am determined to lose more weight, thank you for your support.

Sharon Duxbury
Nanango, QLD Australia

My 8 year old daughter Lisa entered your recipe for Wicked Chocolate cake in the Royal Easter Fair. She entered in the children and student section for chocolate cakes and guess what?! She won first prize!!! The judges had no idea that the cake was low in fat.

Ingrid Player
North Ryde, NSW Australia

14

There are many low-fat cookbooks out these days, but unfortunately they have recipes that a 'normal' family wouldn't eat. Thankyou! Thankyou, for putting out a low fat cookbook with 'normal' recipes.

Janet Wilson
Orange, NSW Australia

Your books are packed with recipes that are mindful of the fact that not everyone can buy exotic ingredients and don't want to spend 4 hours in the kitchen cooking dinner. I was asked how someone can lose weight eating the way I do. I say it is just "Symply Too Good To Be True". I have gone down 4 dress sizes and just couldn't believe how easy it was to lose weight using your recipes. I have to date lost 35lbs.

Linda McGraw
Quaama, NSW Australia

A friend told me about your books and am I glad she did. My doctor advised me to lose some weight and to give up junk food as I weighed 250lbs and ate too much pizza and takeaway meals. Your recipes helped me to lose over 100lbs and I am now a happy and healthy 150lbs. My favourite recipe is your lasagne. Thank you Annette for your quick and easy recipes they really helped me lose the weight and to also keep it off. My husband Jason also thanks you.

Karen Guy
Currimundi, QLD Australia

Since buying your books I have lost 54lbs in 6 months. I thank you for writing such great books; they have not only helped me but my whole family.

Rachel Olsen
Corio, VIC Australia

Since cooking your recipes I have lost 90lbs, almost another person. Thanks to your wonderful books, I have never looked back.

Donna Job
Berwick, VIC Australia

I have been using your cookbooks as bibles for the past 10 months. My sons think I am the best cook in the world and to top it off I have lost 110lbs, my husband has lost 33lbs, and my youngest son has lost 12lbs, I can't thank you enough.

Rhonda Harris
Mackay, QLD Australia

I am a 62 year old male disabled pensioner and I had a weight problem. I was 300lbs and getting heavier all the time. I was told about your cookbooks and since using them I have lost 88lbs in 36 weeks without any exercise. I was border line with a sugar problem but not any more so I am very happy, thank you.

Christopher Smith
Ipswich, QLD Australia

Your cookbooks were recommended to me by my hairdresser who just happened to lose 66lbs with the help of your recipes. Once I discovered Symply too good to be true I kindly donated all my other cookbooks to charity. I also love the fact that every recipe has a picture and in the early days I got very excited that my meals always came out looking as good as the pictures. You have turned me into a great cook and I am proud to tell you that I have now lost 66lbs and my husband Mick has lost 80lbs.

Tanya and Mick
Rochester, VIC Australia

28 Day Weight Loss Plan

This 28 Day Weight Loss Plan has been devised to assist anyone who wants to lose weight the healthy way. So many times people say that dieting is too hard, that they don't know what to eat and how much to have, with most diets being unhealthy and boring. My plan will show you how you can lose weight and still have delicious food including the occasional treat. This is such a healthy plan that it is suitable for people with diabetes. Just follow each day and enjoy the plan, it's that symple.

With a balance of carbohydrates over the day you will find that you won't get the highs and lows that normal dieting gives. It also uses some of the fabulous recipes found in this book SYMPLY TOO GOOD TO BE TRUE, making it easy for you to create the meals required. Most of the recipes can be made ahead of time and can be frozen as well. You then have the convenience of preparing the week ahead if you need to. I tried to keep the days as interesting as possible and easy to follow with a healthy balance of all the food groups. Most diets do not comply with healthy guidelines but this 28 day weight loss plan does. By following this plan you will have enough calcium, fiber, carbohydrates and protein each day, all balanced with a low saturated fat diet. I hope you enjoy the next 28 days and happy slimming.

LEVEL 1 has an average of 30g of fat per day and around 1300 calories.

LEVEL 2 has an average of 40g of fat per day and around 1550 calories.

The intention is for you to lose weight on this Plan, but I highly recommend and encourage you to also include a minimum of 30 minutes exercise at least 4-5 times a week. This way you will get the full benefit of this weight loss plan.

WHICH LEVEL SHOULD I BE ON?

LEVEL 1
- If you want quick weight loss
- Have only a few pounds to lose
- Do not do a lot of exercise
- Are elderly and not very mobile

LEVEL 2
- If you have 25-30lbs or more to lose
- If you are a very active female
- If you are an inactive male

This 28 Day Weight Loss Plan is not suitable for children, pregnant or breastfeeding women. There is not enough food on this plan for men unless they are inactive and need to lose less than 20lbs in weight.

Annette Sym takes no responsibility or liability for anyone who chooses to follow the plan. Please consult your doctor before embarking on any diet.

What Is The Difference Between Level 1 And Level 2?

LEVEL 1
This level is for a woman who is inactive or has less than 20lbs to lose. The average daily intake is around 30g of fat and 1300 calories. If you have only a few pounds to lose it will be important that you follow the plan exactly as is and make sure you include some form of exercise at least 4 times a week.

LEVEL 1
You must eat what is listed for BREAKFAST, LUNCH, DINNER and SNACKS as in LEVEL 1 only for each day. You don't get to have the extra section called LEVEL 2.

LEVEL 2
This level is for a woman who is reasonably active or who has more than 20-30lbs to lose. It would also be suitable for an inactive man. The average daily intake is around 40g of fat and 1500 calories.

LEVEL 2
You must eat what is listed for BREAKFAST, LUNCH, DINNER and SNACKS in LEVEL 1 plus you get to have what is listed in the LEVEL 2 section for each day.

Do not miss any of the food listed as it may cause you to be hungry the following day. You cannot swap any choices from one day to another and you must only eat what is on the list for that day. Eating more than what is listed on the daily menu may jeopardize your weight loss.

SALAD & VEGETABLES
Salad and vegetables are unlimited but please have at least what is suggested in the menu. Salad consists of lettuce, tomato, cucumber, bell peppers, onion, sprouts, beetroot, celery, carrot. It does not include avocado or corn. Vegetables include all vegetable varieties except potato, sweet potato and corn. If you are to have any of these choices they will be listed separately.

BREAD/CARBOHYDRATES
Whole wheat or grain bread and bread rolls are used in this plan as they have a lower Glycemic Index. If you have a gluten or wheat intolerance replace bread with gluten free bread that weighs no more than 1oz a slice and replace pasta with rice pasta.

Rice should be basmati rice as it too has a lower Glycemic Index.

DRINKS
Wherever you see no-fat milk in the menu plan please use calcium fortified milk as it increases the calcium intake for each day. Use milk allocated in the snacks section for tea and coffee or as a drink. If you are lactose intolerant then use no fat soy milk. I would recommend that you have only a couple of cups of coffee or tea each day unless de-caffeinated. Diet soda drinks are allowed as long as they are de-caffeinated. Alcohol has not been included in the menus, if you wish to include alcohol be aware that you are adding extra calories to your day which may slow your weight loss down. You must drink at least 8 glasses of water every day.

TIPS
Don't guess the weights of food such as 4oz chicken. I would suggest you invest in a small set of digital scales so your portions are accurate. If you don't want one of the choices that are in this cookbook then check the calories and fat count of the recipe per serve and if you wish you can swap it for another recipe from this cookbook as long as the recipe you choose has a similar fat and calorie count. The same goes for other items such as swapping ham as your lunch choice: just swap for another lean meat that has a similar fat and calorie count, such as turkey.

The most important part of this plan is the weighing and measuring of food choices. This will show where you may have been over-consuming without even knowing it. I remember the first time I weighed 3oz of cooked chicken, I was amazed how small it was and quickly realized that I had been eating way more than I should have, which may explain why I weighed 220lbs. As you progress you will get familiar with how much the food you eat weighs, but to start with be diligent when it comes to weighing and measuring your food.

		Day 1	Day 2	Day 3	
LEVEL 1	**Breakfast**	¾ cup Heart Smart Kellogg's® or other high fiber cereal ½ cup no-fat milk 5oz fresh fruit	1 slice whole wheat bread toasted ½ cup baked beans 1 small tomato 2oz mushrooms	½ cup All Bran® cereal 1 cup no-fat milk 5oz fresh fruit	
	Lunch	4 Ryvita or Wasa® crispbread 1 slice sharp 2% milk reduced fat cheese 1oz lean ham 1 cup salad 1 tsp light margarine 5oz fresh pear	1oz deli sliced turkey 2 slices whole wheat bread 2 tsp mayonnaise 80% less fat 2 cups salad 1½oz avocado 5oz fresh fruit	2oz bagel whole wheat 1oz lean ham 1oz cream cheese ⅓ less fat 2 cups salad 1½oz Lays® potato chips	
	Dinner	1 serve Fish Alaska PAGE 84 5oz boiled potato (with skin on) 2 cups vegetables or salad	1 serve Chicken Pizziola PAGE 100 2 cups vegetables or salad 1 tub 6oz no-fat fruit yogurt	1 serve Macaroni Beef PAGE 122 1 cup salad	
	Snacks	1 cup no-fat milk 1 tub 6oz no-fat fruit yogurt 20 almonds	1 cup no-fat milk 6oz fresh strawberries 3 Pikelets PAGE 218 1 tsp jam 1 tsp light margarine	1 cup no-fat milk 5oz fresh apple 1 chocolate fudge ice cream bar (Weight Watchers®)	
LEVEL 2	**Extras**	4 Pikelets PAGE 218 2 tsp jam 10 more almonds	1oz more turkey (lunch) ½oz more avocado (lunch) 2 extra pikelets 1 tsp jam 2 tsp light margarine (allow 1 tsp for b'fast)	5oz fresh fruit ¼ cup more All Bran (breakfast) ½oz more Lays® potato chips (lunch) ½oz more bagel (lunch)	

Day 4	Day 5	Day 6	Day 7
½ cup All Bran® cereal ½ cup no-fat milk 5oz fresh fruit	2 squares (4") waffles ¼ cup maple syrup sugar free 1 cup no-fat milk	1 cup cooked rolled oats ½ cup no-fat milk 1 slice raisin toast 1 tsp light margarine	2oz bagel whole wheat toasted 1oz cream cheese ⅓ less fat ½ cup no-fat milk
7oz (2 slices) Pizza-meat & veg thin crust low fat (frozen pre-made) 1 cup salad ¾oz avocado	1 boiled egg 2oz Canadian lean bacon (raw) 2 cups salad 1 tbsp mayonnaise 80% less fat 1oz peanuts 5oz fresh fruit 1 cup no-fat milk	1 serve Chinese Omelette PAGE 138 1 cup salad 1 tub 6oz no-fat fruit yogurt 1 chocolate fudge ice cream bar (Weight Watchers®)	1oz shredded sharp 2% milk reduced fat cheese 2oz deli sliced turkey 2 cups salad 1 tbsp mayonnaise 80% less fat 5oz fresh pear
1 serve Homestead Chicken Pie PAGE 106 4oz boiled potato 2 cups vegetables or salad	1 serve Garlic Shrimp PAGE 86 ½ cup cooked basmati rice 2 cups vegetables or salad	4oz roast pork (lean) 1 serve Baked Vegetables PAGE 44 1 cup vegetables ¼ cup made up gravy (French's brown gravy mix ®) 5oz fresh fruit	1 serve Bolognaise PAGE 151 1 tsp parmesan cheese 1 cup cooked pasta 2 cups vegetables or salad
1 cup no-fat milk 1 serve Pear & Cranberry Loaf PAGE 214 5oz watermelon or strawberries	1 cup no-fat milk 1 chocolate fudge ice cream bar (Weight Watchers®) 8oz strawberries	1 cup no-fat milk 1 serve Pear & Cranberry loaf PAGE 214 5oz fresh fruit	1 cup no-fat milk 1oz popcorn (94% fat-free microwave) 6oz watermelon
2oz more pizza (lunch) ¼oz more avocado (lunch) 5oz fresh fruit	¼ cup more cooked rice (dinner) 1oz more peanuts	1oz cashews 5oz fresh fruit	1½oz milk or dark chocolate

		Day 8	Day 9	Day 10	
LEVEL 1	**Breakfast**	1 egg 1 tomato 1 cup raw sliced mushrooms (pan fried in non-stick pan with cooking spray) 1 slice whole wheat toast 1 tsp light margarine 6oz fresh fruit	¾ cup Heart Smart Kellogg's® or other high fiber cereal ¾ cup no-fat milk 6oz strawberries	1 cup Heart Smart Kellogg's® or other high fiber cereal ¾ cup no-fat milk	
	Lunch	1 serve Minestrone Soup PAGE 33 6 whole wheat crackers (reduced fat) 5oz fresh fruit	2 slices whole wheat bread 2oz cooked chicken breast 2 cups salad 2oz avocado 5oz fresh pear	1 serve Minestrone Soup PAGE 33 2 slices whole wheat bread 1½oz roast beef (Hillshire Farm Deli Select®) 1 cup salad 1oz avocado 1 tsp light margarine	
	Dinner	2 Fish Fillets (Crisp & Healthy Breaded - Van De Kamp's®) 2 cups salad 1 serve Oven Baked Fries PAGE 50 1 tub 6oz no-fat fruit yogurt	1 serve Mild Sweet Curry PAGE 125 ½ cup cooked basmati rice	3 Tacos PAGE 59 1 tub 6oz no-fat fruit yogurt	
	Snacks	1½ cups no-fat milk 1 chocolate fudge ice cream bar (Weight Watchers®) 1½oz light corn chips (⅓ fewer calories)	1 cup no-fat milk 5oz fresh fruit 1 chocolate fudge ice cream bar (Weight Watchers®)	1 cup no-fat milk 6oz strawberries 5oz fresh fruit	
LEVEL 2	**Extras**	1 extra egg (b'fast) 1 extra fish fillet (dinner) ½oz more light corn chips (⅓ fewer calories)	1½oz light corn chips (⅓ fewer calories)	1½oz milk or dark chocolate	

Day 11	Day 12	Day 13	Day 14
1 slice whole wheat toast ¾ cup spaghetti (canned) 1 slice sharp 2% milk reduced fat cheese	1 square (4") waffle 1oz maple syrup sugar free 5oz fresh fruit	¾ cup Wheaties® or other high fiber cereal ¾ cup no-fat milk 5oz fresh fruit	¾ cup cooked rolled oats ¾ cup no-fat milk 5oz fresh fruit
3oz canned pink salmon 2 cups salad 1 tbsp mayonnaise 80% less fat 1oz avocado 5oz fresh fruit 1 tub 6oz no-fat fruit yogurt	2 Tacos PAGE 59 1oz avocado 1 serve Chocolate Slice PAGE 206	3oz pita bread 1oz deli sliced turkey 1 slice sharp 2% milk reduced-fat cheese 2 cups salad 2 tsp mayonnaise 80% less fat 5oz fresh pear	1 serve Creamy Chicken & Vegetable Soup PAGE 29 4 whole wheat crackers (reduced fat) 5oz fresh pear
4oz raw steak (broiled) 1 serve Oven Baked Fries PAGE 50 1 cup of vegetables 1 cup cooked spinach 2 tsp BBQ sauce	1 serve Shepherd's Pie PAGE 127 5oz strawberries or watermelon	1 serve Tuna Patties PAGE 90 2 cups vegetables or salad 1 serve Chocolate Slice PAGE 206	1 serve Shepherd's Pie PAGE 127 1 cup vegetables
1 cup no-fat milk 5oz fresh fruit 1 serve Chocolate Slice PAGE 206	1 cup no-fat milk 1 tub 6oz no-fat fruit yogurt 2 Ryvita or Wasa® crispbread 1 slice sharp 2% milk reduced fat cheese 1 tomato	½ cup no-fat milk 30 almonds 1 tub 6oz no-fat fruit yogurt	1 cup no-fat milk 5oz fresh fruit 30 almonds
2 slices whole wheat bread (lunch) 1oz more avocado (lunch) 1oz more raw steak (dinner)	1 extra square (4") waffle (breakfast) 1 extra Taco (lunch) ½oz more avocado (lunch)	1 extra Tuna Patty (dinner) 3oz boiled potato (dinner) 15 more almonds	1½oz milk or dark chocolate

		Day 15	Day 16	Day 17
LEVEL 1	**Breakfast**	¾ cup All Bran® cereal ¾ cup no-fat milk 5oz fresh fruit	2½oz bagel whole wheat 1oz cream cheese ⅓ less fat	¾ cup Wheaties® or other high fiber cereal ¾ cup no-fat milk 5oz fresh fruit
	Lunch	1 serve Tuna Patties PAGE 90 2 cups vegetables or salad 1 slice whole wheat bread 1 tsp light margarine	1 serve Creamy Chicken & Vegetable Soup PAGE 29 4 whole wheat crackers (reduced fat)	2½oz bagel whole wheat 1oz shredded sharp 2% milk reduced-fat cheese 1oz lean ham 1oz fresh pineapple 2 cups salad
	Dinner	7oz (2 slices) Pizza-meat & veg thin crust low fat (frozen pre-made) 2 cups salad	4oz raw pork leg steak lean (grilled) 5oz boiled potatoes 2 cups mixed vegetables or salad 5oz fresh fruit	1 serve Chicken Cashew Stir Fry PAGE 135 ½ cup cooked basmati rice ½oz cashews 6oz fresh pear
	Snacks	1 cup no-fat milk 1 serve Creamy Coconut Rice PAGE 183 6oz strawberries or watermelon	1 cup no-fat milk 5oz fresh fruit 1oz peanuts	1 cup no-fat milk 8oz strawberries or watermelon 3oz 98% fat-free ice cream(Breyers®)
LEVEL 2	**Extras**	1 slice whole wheat bread (lunch) 1oz extra avocado 2oz more pizza (dinner)	½oz more bagel (breakfast) 2 extra crackers (lunch) 1oz more raw pork leg steak lean (dinner) 5oz fresh fruit ½oz more peanuts	1½oz Lays® potato chips

Day 18	Day 19	Day 20	Day 21
3 egg white omelette 1oz shredded sharp 2% milk reduced fat cheese 1oz lean ham 2 slices whole wheat toast 1 tsp light margarine 5oz fresh fruit	1 fruit bran muffin (Jennies Cuisine®) 1 cup no-fat milk	¾ cup All Bran® cereal ¾ cup no-fat milk 5oz fresh fruit	1 cup Wheaties® or other high fiber cereal ½ cup no-fat milk 6oz strawberries
3oz pita bread 2oz canned pink salmon (drained) 2 cups salad 2 tsp mayonnaise 80% less fat	1 serve Rippa Rissole PAGE 130 2 cups salad 2 tsp mayonnaise 80% less fat 5oz fresh fruit	1 Turkey Burger Patty (Jennie-O®) 2½oz whole wheat bun 1 cup salad 1 tsp mayonnaise 80% less fat	1 serve Chilli Beef PAGE 61 1oz light corn chips (⅓ fewer calories) 1 cup salad
1 serve Rippa Rissoles PAGE 130 ¼ cup made up gravy (French's® brown gravy mix) 5oz boiled potato 1 cup vegetables 1 cup spinach	5oz raw fish fillets (pan fry with cooking spray) 1 serve Oven Baked Fries PAGE 50 2 cups vegetables or salad	1 serve Chilli Beef PAGE 61 1oz light corn chips (⅓ fewer calories) 1oz shredded sharp 2% milk reduced fat cheese	1 serve Pizza Strudel PAGE 67 2 cups vegetables or salad 5oz boiled potato 6oz strawberries or watermelon
1 cup no-fat milk 6oz strawberries or watermelon 20 almonds	1 cup no-fat milk 5oz fresh fruit 30 almonds	1 cup no-fat milk 5oz fresh fruit 3 chocolate chip reduced fat cookies (Nabisco®)	1 cup no-fat milk 30 almonds 1 tub 6oz no-fat fruit yogurt
½oz more salmon 1oz more boiled potato 10 more almonds 3oz 98% fat-free ice cream (Breyers®)	1 extra serve Oven Baked Fries 15 more almonds	½oz more corn chips 1oz avocado (lunch or dinner) 3oz 98% fat-free ice cream (Breyers®)	½ serve more Pizza Strudel PAGE 67 3 reduced fat chocolate chip cookies (Nabisco®)

		Day 22	Day 23	Day 24
LEVEL 1	**Breakfast**	1 Fruit Bran muffin (Jennies Cuisine®) 5oz fresh fruit	½ cup All Bran cereal ¾ cup no-fat milk 5oz fresh fruit	½ cup All Bran cereal 1 cup no-fat milk 5oz fresh fruit
	Lunch	1 serve Pizza Strudel PAGE 67 2 cups vegetables or salad 1 tub 6oz no-fat fruit yogurt	2oz bagel whole wheat 1oz roast beef (deli select) 2 cups salad 2 tsp mayonnaise 80% less fat 1 tub 6oz no-fat fruit yogurt	1 serve Potato & Leek Soup PAGE 36 5 whole wheat crackers (reduced fat) 1 serve Fruit 'n' Nut Cobbler PAGE 185
	Dinner	1 serve Beef Stroganoff PAGE 117 ½ cup cooked basmati rice 2 cups vegetables or salad	2 pork sausages reduced fat (Jimmy Deans®) 2 tsp BBQ sauce 1 serve Oven Baked Fries PAGE 50 2 cups vegetables or salad	1 serve Mexican Chicken Stack PAGE 112 1 cup salad 1oz avocado 1 x 3 Musketeers® Mint Bar 45% less fat (35.2g)
	Snacks	1 cup no-fat milk 5oz watermelon 2 reduced fat chocolate chip cookies (Nabisco®) 20 almonds	1 cup no-fat milk 1 serve Fruit 'n' Nut Cobbler PAGE 185 5oz strawberries or watermelon	1 cup no-fat milk 5oz watermelon 2 Ryvitas or Wasa® crispbread 1 tbsp peanut butter
LEVEL 2	**Extras**	½ cup more no-fat milk 10 more almonds 2 reduced fat chocolate chip cookies (Nabisco®) ¼ cup more rice (dinner)	1 extra sausage 1 extra serve Oven Baked Fries	¼ cup more All Bran® cereal ½ cup more no-fat milk 2 extra Ryvita or Wasa® crispbread 1 tbsp peanut butter

Day 25	Day 26	Day 27	Day 28
2 Weetabix or ¾ cup high fiber cereal 1 cup no-fat milk 5oz fresh fruit	1 Fruit Bran muffin (Jennies Cuisine®) ½ cup no-fat milk	2 Weetabix or ¾ cup high fiber cereal ¾ cup no-fat milk 5oz fresh fruit	1 poached egg 1 small tomato 2oz raw mushrooms (all pan fried in non stick pan with cooking spray) 2 slices whole wheat toast 1 tsp light margarine 5oz fresh banana
1oz deli sliced turkey 2 slices whole wheat bread 2 tsp mayonnaise 80% less fat 1½oz avocado 2 cups salad 5oz fresh fruit	1 serve Potato & Leek Soup PAGE 36 5 whole wheat crackers (reduced fat) 5oz fresh fruit	7oz (2 slices) Pizza-meat & veg thin crust low fat (frozen pre-made) 2 cups salad	4 Ryvita or Wasa® crispbread 2 slices sharp 2% milk reduced-fat cheese 2 cups salad 1 tsp light margarine
1 serve Lasagne PAGE 118 2 cups salad	1 serve Chicken Pesto Pasta PAGE 154 2 cups salad 2oz Breyers 98% fat-free ice cream	4oz fresh salmon portion (pan fried with cooking spray) 5oz boiled potato 1½ cups vegetables ½ cup cooked spinach	1 Turkey Burger PAGE 77 (no bun) 7oz potato 2 cups vegetables or salad
1 cup no-fat milk 5oz fresh fruit 1 serve Fruit 'n' Nut Cobbler PAGE 185	1 cup no-fat milk 5oz fresh fruit 1½oz light corn chips (⅓ fewer calorie)	1 cup no-fat milk 1½oz popcorn (94% fat-free microwave) 5oz fresh apple	1 cup no-fat milk 5oz fresh fruit 1 chocolate fudge ice cream bar (Weight Watchers®)
1½oz Lays® potato chips	1½oz avocado with salad ½oz more light corn chips (⅓ fewer calories) 5oz fresh fruit	2oz more pizza (lunch) 2oz more boiled potato ½oz more popcorn	2oz light corn chips (⅓ fewer calories)

Soups and Salads

CAESAR SALAD

Makes 4 servings

Dressing

1 egg

½ cup 80% less fat mayonnaise (Best Foods®)

4 anchovy fillets

1 tablespoon grated parmesan cheese

1 tablespoon fresh chopped parsley

2 tablespoons water

Croutons

3 slices whole wheat bread

cooking spray

Salad

¾ cup Canadian style bacon 95% fat free

1 large green leaf lettuce

1 x 8oz punnet cherry tomatoes cut in half

1 tablespoon grated parmesan cheese

To make 1 cup of Dressing: Boil egg for 5 minutes, cool slightly then shell. Place all ingredients except egg into food processor or blender, blend for 30 seconds. Add egg, blend for 10-15 seconds.

To make Croutons: Heat oven to 400°F (200°C) fan forced. Toast bread, then cut into small cubes, place bread on baking tray. Lightly coat with cooking spray then bake for 10-15 minutes, or until brown and hard.

To make Salad: Cut bacon into small cubes then coat a non-stick frypan with cooking spray, fry bacon until cooked. Drain on paper towel. Wash lettuce leaves, break into chunks and place in a large salad bowl. Scatter tomatoes and bacon over lettuce. Add ½ cup dressing (refrigerate remaining dressing for another time). Toss ingredients together. Sprinkle croutons and cheese on top.

Variation: Chicken Caesar Salad - Replace bacon with 8oz raw skinless chicken breast, pan fried with cooking spray then sliced.

Not suitable to be frozen.

Nutritional Information

PER SERVE	CAESAR	CHICKEN
CALORIES	158	194
TOTAL FAT	6.7g	7.1g
SATURATED FAT	1.5g	1.5g
SODIUM	663mg	435mg
CARBS	12.8g	12.8g
SUGAR	5.5g	5.5g
FIBER	4.2g	4.2g
PROTEIN	11.5g	20.1g
GI RATING	Low	Low

Dietitian's tip
At last a Caesar salad that is low in calories and saturated fat, making this a great choice for people with diabetes who want to lose weight.

CREAMY CHICKEN & VEGETABLE SOUP

Makes 8 servings

cooking spray

2 teaspoons crushed garlic (in jar)

14oz skinless chicken breast

1 cup onion diced

1 cup carrot diced

1 cup frozen peas

1 cup frozen corn kernels

4 cups water

2 tablespoons granulated chicken bouillon (low sodium)

½ teaspoon dried tarragon

½ cup uncooked macaroni pasta

2½ cups no-fat milk

1 x 12½oz can low-fat 2% evaporated milk

2 tablespoons fresh chopped parsley

pepper

Cut chicken into small dice. In a boiler or stock pot that has been generously coated with cooking spray, sauté garlic and chicken for 1 minute. Add onion and carrots and cook 1 minute. Add peas and corn, cook 1 minute more.

Add water, bouillon and tarragon, bring to boil. Add pasta stirring in well, bring to boil. Reduce to a medium boil for 20 minutes, stirring occasionally. Add no-fat milk, evaporated milk and parsley. Add pepper to taste, stir in well. Once boiled serve.

Variation: Replace chicken breast with skinless turkey breast.

Suitable to be frozen for 2-3 weeks.

Nutritional Information

PER SERVE

CALORIES	195
TOTAL FAT	2.2g
SATURATED FAT	0.6g
SODIUM	187mg
CARBS	26.6g
SUGAR	13.0g
FIBER	3.3g
PROTEIN	20.9g
GI RATING	Low

Dietitian's tip

A creamy soup packed with protein, vitamins and minerals and still low in fat. Thanks Annette.

CRUNCHY NOODLE SALAD

Makes 10 servings as a side dish

⅓ cup slivered almonds

2 tablespoons sesame seeds

½ cup 100% fat-free Italian dressing (Kraft®)

1 tablespoon soy sauce (low sodium)

⅓ cup dark brown sugar

1 small Chinese cabbage shredded

¾ cup celery sliced

½ cup green onions chopped

2 cups crispy chow mein noodles

Place almonds onto a flat baking tray that is covered with aluminum foil and brown under the griller. Be careful as they burn easily. Remove and leave to one side. Place sesame seeds under griller like almonds and brown, they brown very quickly so keep an eye on them then place to one side.

In a small container place dressing, soy sauce and dark brown sugar, put lid on securely and shake until sugar has dissolved. Place shredded cabbage, sliced celery and green onions in a large serving bowl.

When ready to serve toss the noodles, sesame seeds, almonds and dressing together with the cabbage. You leave this to the last minute as the noodles soften quickly.

Not suitable to be frozen.

Nutritional Information

PER SERVE

CALORIES	116
TOTAL FAT	5.2g
SATURATED FAT	0.6g
SODIUM	231mg
CARBS	13.0g
SUGAR	5.9g
FIBER	2.4g
PROTEIN	3.8g
GI RATING	Low

Dietitian's tip
This is a great recipe that allows diet-conscious people to enjoy the healthy benefits of nuts. Almonds are rich in healthy mono-unsaturated fats.

MINESTRONE SOUP

Makes 8 servings

8 cups water

1 cup celery sliced

1 cup small broccoli florets

1 cup zucchini diced

1 cup peeled potato diced

1 cup onion chopped

1 x 14oz can no-salt-added diced tomatoes

1 x 15½oz can kidney beans drained and washed

½ cup uncooked macaroni pasta

½ cup no-salt-added tomato paste

4 teaspoons granulated beef bouillon (low sodium)

1 teaspoon crushed garlic (in jar)

1 teaspoon dried basil

1 teaspoon dried oregano

½ cup fresh chopped parsley

pepper

Place all ingredients into a boiler or large saucepan. Bring to boil then simmer 20-25 minutes or until vegetables are tender. Stir occasionally to avoid pasta sticking to bottom of pan. Add pepper to taste.

Suitable to be frozen.

Nutritional Information

PER SERVE

CALORIES	82
TOTAL FAT	0.7g
SATURATED FAT	0.1g
SODIUM	283mg
CARBS	14.7g
SUGAR	6.2g
FIBER	5.5g
PROTEIN	5.2g
GI RATING	Medium

Dietitian's tip

This soup has loads of vegetables that provide essential vitamins and minerals for repairing body cells.

DELUXE POTATO SALAD
Makes 8 servings as a side dish

1½lbs potatoes

1½lbs sweet potatoes

½ cup red onion sliced or ½ cup green onions finely sliced

2 tablespoons fresh mint finely chopped

½ cup light sour cream

¼ cup ranch dressing fat free (Kraft®)

pepper

Peel both potatoes and cut into cubes (about 1"). Microwave in a little water for 15 to 20 minutes or until just cooked through. Once cooked, turn into a colander and run cold water over potato for a few minutes. Leave to drain. Cut onion in quarters and slice finely.

Place potato and onion into a large mixing bowl. In a small mixing bowl combine mint, sour cream and ranch dressing. Add dressing to potato and fold gently until combined. Add pepper to taste.

Variation: Replace sweet potato with plain potato for a traditional potato salad.

Not suitable to be frozen.

Nutritional Information

PER SERVE	
CALORIES	136
TOTAL FAT	1.1g
SATURATED FAT	0.5g
SODIUM	113mg
CARBS	26.2g
SUGAR	7.3g
FIBER	3.1g
PROTEIN	4.7g
GI RATING	Medium

Dietitian's tip

The use of sweet potato in this recipe lowers the Glycemic Index.

POTATO & LEEK SOUP

Makes 8 servings

1 large leek

2 tablespoons light margarine (Promise®)

2 tablespoons all purpose flour

4 cups water

2½ cups no-fat milk

6 cups potato peeled and diced

2 tablespoons granulated chicken or vegetable bouillon (low sodium)

1 x 12½oz can low-fat 2% evaporated milk

pepper

Cut leek lengthways into 2 pieces and wash well, cut into slices, measuring around 3 cups. Melt margarine in a boiler or large pot, add leeks and cook 1 minute. Add in the flour and cook 1 minute. Slowly add in water and no-fat milk stirring continuously. Bring to boil then add diced potato and bouillon.

Simmer for 30 minutes with lid on, stir occasionally to prevent mixture from sticking. Pour in evaporated milk and bring back to boil. Reduce to a simmer and cook a further 5 minutes. Mash soup until a fairly smooth consistency is achieved. Add pepper to taste.

Suitable to be frozen for 2-3 weeks.

Nutritional Information

PER SERVE

CALORIES	173
TOTAL FAT	2.0g
SATURATED FAT	0.4g
SODIUM	145mg
CARBS	30.5g
SUGAR	12.2g
FIBER	3.3g
PROTEIN	9.9g
GI RATING	Medium

Dietitian's tip

This is a great choice for people wanting a tasty soup without the added sodium (salt). Ideal for those with high blood pressure.

THAI BEEF NOODLE SALAD

Makes 4 servings

Dressing

¼ cup fresh lime juice

¼ cup water

½ teaspoon crushed garlic (in jar)

½ teaspoon crushed ginger (in jar)

2 teaspoons soy sauce (low sodium)

1 tablespoon Pad Thai sauce

1 teaspoon Thai red curry paste

2 teaspoons lemon grass chopped (in jar)

1 tablespoon fresh cilantro leaves chopped

1 tablespoon sugar

Salad

4oz thin rice noodles

1lb lean beef steak

cooking spray

4 cups lettuce

20 slices cucumber

20 cherry tomatoes cut in half

¾ cup bell peppers sliced

1 carrot thinly sliced

16 snow peas thinly sliced on angle

½ cup green onion thinly sliced on angle

To make dressing: Place all dressing ingredients in a small mixing bowl, use a whisk to blend well.

To make salad: Cook noodles by following the instructions on packet. Divide salad ingredients equally over 4 dinner plates. In a non-stick frypan that has been generously coated with cooking spray, fry beef until cooked to your liking. Cut into thin strips and leave to one side. Place noodles on top of salad then put steak slices over top. Pour dressing over salad and serve.

Variations: Replace beef with lean lamb steaks, skinless chicken breasts or peeled raw shrimp.

Not suitable to be frozen.

Nutritional Information				
PER SERVE	BEEF	LAMB	CHICKEN	SHRIMP
CALORIES	249	240	230	213
TOTAL FAT	5.0g	4.8g	3.3g	1.4g
SATURATED FAT	1.7g	1.9g	0.8g	0.2g
SODIUM	272mg	290mg	264mg	598mg
CARBS	19.8g	19.8g	19.8g	19.8g
SUGAR	9.1g	9.1g	9.1g	9.1g
FIBER	3.4g	3.4g	3.4g	3.4g
PROTEIN	28.5g	28.4g	29.0g	27.9g
GI RATING	Low	Low	Low	Low

Dietitian's tip
The shrimp variation is high in sodium (salt) compared to the meat. Choose this option on special occasions or pick the other variations instead.

SEAFOOD CHOWDER
Makes 8 servings

2 cups water

½ cup white wine

1 teaspoon crushed garlic (in jar)

2 teaspoons fish sauce

10oz boneless fish fillets
cut into pieces

½ cup green onions chopped

5oz peeled raw shrimp

2oz seafood flakes

1 x 6oz can crabmeat drained

2 tablespoons fresh
chopped parsley

5 tablespoons cornstarch

2 cups no-fat milk

1 x 12½oz can low-fat
2% evaporated milk

pepper

In a large boiler place water, wine, garlic and fish sauce. Bring to boil, add fish and cook for 2 minutes. Add green onions, shrimp, seafood flakes, canned crabmeat and parsley. Simmer for 5 minutes. In a cup mix cornstarch with ½ cup of the no-fat milk, leave to one side. Using another saucepan pour the remaining 1½ cups of no-fat milk and whole can of evaporated milk together.

Once boiled pour into boiler (I have done it this way as the milk will scorch if you boil it with the seafood), now add in remaining milk and cornstarch mix and bring to boil. Take off quickly so as not to let the bottom of the pan scorch. Add pepper to taste.

Suitable to be frozen for 2-3 weeks.

Nutritional Information

PER SERVE	
CALORIES	148
TOTAL FAT	1.5g
SATURATED FAT	0.3g
SODIUM	411mg
CARBS	13.4g
SUGAR	8.2g
FIBER	0.1g
PROTEIN	17.5g
GI RATING	Low

Dietitian's tip

A creamy chowder minus the fat – well done Annette!

BEANS 'N' BACON

Makes 6 servings as a side dish

1lb fresh green beans

cooking spray

½ teaspoon crushed garlic (in jar)

½ cup onion finely diced

3oz Canadian Style 95% fat-free bacon diced

2 tablespoons no-salt-added tomato paste

Trim ends off beans. In a microwave-safe dish microwave in a little water until beans are cooked to your liking. Drain. Coat a non-stick frypan with cooking spray, sauté garlic, onion and bacon until cooked. Add tomato paste and cooked beans, toss until beans are coated with sauce.

Suitable to be frozen.

Nutritional Information

PER SERVE	
CALORIES	40
TOTAL FAT	0.8g
SATURATED FAT	0.3g
SODIUM	180mg
CARBS	2.7g
SUGAR	1.7g
FIBER	2.2g
PROTEIN	4.9g
GI RATING	Too low in carbs to score a rating

Dietitian's tip

Microwave the beans for a short time to retain the water-soluble vitamins.

BAKED VEGETABLES

Makes 4 servings

4 medium size potatoes

4 x 4oz pieces pumpkin or butternut squash

4 medium size carrots

4 small onions

cooking spray

Preheat oven to 475°F (230°C) fan forced.

Peel vegetables. Cut potatoes in half and pumpkin into large pieces. Keep carrots and onions whole. If onions are large then cut in half and use only 2 onions. In a microwave-safe dish microwave vegetables in a little water for 10 minutes on high, then drain.

Coat baking pan generously with cooking spray. Place vegetables in pan, generously spray over top of vegetables. Bake on top rack 30-40 minutes or until golden brown, turning once.

Variations: Other vegetables that bake well are sweet potato, turnip, parsnip, beetroot and rutabaga (swede).

Not suitable to be frozen.

Nutritional Information

PER SERVE	
CALORIES	102
TOTAL FAT	0.4g
SATURATED FAT	0.1g
SODIUM	36mg
CARBS	20.3g
SUGAR	8.3g
FIBER	6.1g
PROTEIN	4.3g
GI RATING	Medium

Dietitian's tip
A fabulously tasty way to have low-fat baked vegetables. Great for preventing chronic diseases such as diabetes, heart disease and some types of cancers.

STUFFED MUSHROOMS

Makes 6 servings as a side dish

1 cup cooked basmati rice

½ cup tomato finely diced

½ cup onion finely diced

½ cup celery finely diced

½ cup bell peppers finely diced

½ teaspoon crushed garlic (in jar)

1 tablespoon barbeque sauce

1 teaspoon Worcestershire sauce

1 tablespoon tomato ketchup

2 tablespoons grated parmesan cheese

½ teaspoon dried oregano

½ teaspoon granulated vegetable or beef bouillon (low sodium)

18 medium size mushrooms

cooking spray

½ cup shredded sharp 2% milk reduced-fat cheese

Preheat oven to 350°F (180ºC) fan forced.

In a large mixing bowl combine all ingredients except mushrooms and shredded cheese. Remove stem from mushrooms and spoon filling into each cap. Place each mushroom on a flat baking pan coated with cooking spray. Sprinkle a little cheese over top of each mushroom, bake for 25 minutes.

Variations: Add to filling 2oz Canadian style bacon 95% fat-free finely diced. Or replace mushrooms with 3 large zucchinis. Cut zucchinis in half lengthways and scoop out soft centre. Put stuffing into zucchinis and sprinkle cheese over top, bake 35 minutes.

Not suitable to be frozen.

Nutritional Information

PER SERVE	MUSHROOM	BACON	ZUCCHINI
CALORIES	92	104	97
TOTAL FAT	3.1g	3.5g	3.2g
SATURATED FAT	1.7g	1.8g	1.7g
SODIUM	231mg	342mg	230mg
CARBS	10.9g	10.8g	11.7g
SUGAR	3.0g	3.0g	4.5g
FIBER	1.7g	1.7g	2.4g
PROTEIN	5.8g	7.7g	5.7g
GI RATING	Medium	Medium	Medium

Dietitian's tip

A tasty dish to serve as an appetizer or at a barbeque. The use of basmati rice lowers the Glycemic Index of this dish.

LENTIL HOTPOT

Makes 4 large servings or 8 as a side dish

1 cup onion diced

1 teaspoon crushed garlic (in jar)

cooking spray

1 teaspoon ground cumin

1 teaspoon ground cilantro

1 teaspoon crushed ginger (in jar)

1 teaspoon ground turmeric

2 teaspoons granulated vegetable bouillon (low sodium)

2 cups boiling water

2 cups raw pumpkin or butternut squash diced

2 cups raw potato diced

1 cup green beans cut in half

¾ cup dried red lentils

1 x 14oz can no-salt-added diced tomatoes

Sauté onion and garlic for 2 minutes in large saucepan that has been generously coated with cooking spray. Combine cumin, cilantro, ginger and turmeric with onion, sauté 1 minute.

Dissolve bouillon in boiling water, pour into saucepan. Add all other ingredients, bring to boil, cover and simmer slowly for 25-30 minutes or until lentils and potatoes are cooked, stir occasionally.

Suitable to be frozen.

Nutritional Information

PER SERVE	LARGE	SIDE DISH
CALORIES	207	104
TOTAL FAT	1.4g	0.7g
SATURATED FAT	0.4g	0.3g
SODIUM	63mg	32mg
CARBS	35.3g	17.7g
SUGAR	9.1g	4.5g
FIBER	10.3g	5.1g
PROTEIN	14.4g	7.2g
GI RATING	Medium	Medium

Dietitian's tip

Lentils contain protein and low Glycaemic Index carbohydrate. A great combination for vegetarian or vegan people and ideal for people with diabetes.

OVEN BAKED FRIES

Makes 4 servings

4 x 8oz potatoes

cooking spray

Preheat oven to 475°F (230°C) fan forced.

Peel and cut potatoes into fries. Microwave on high for 8 minutes in a little water, drain well. Coat surface of a flat baking pan generously with cooking spray then place fries on pan. Generously spray over fries with cooking spray. Bake on top rack for 35-40 minutes or until golden brown, turn once.

Variation: Replace potato with sweet potato, but note that sweet potato cooks quicker than normal potato.

Not suitable to be frozen.

Nutritional Information

PER SERVE	POTATO	SWEET POTATO
CALORIES	118	122
TOTAL FAT	0.4g	0.4g
SATURATED FAT	0.1g	0.1g
SODIUM	6mg	21mg
CARBS	24.0g	26.4g
SUGAR	0.7g	10.5g
FIBER	3.6g	4.3g
PROTEIN	4.7g	3.6g
GI RATING	High	Low

Dietitian's tip
A great way to cook fries that are low in both total and saturated fats. This makes them ideal for people with diabetes who are overweight. Sweet potato has a low Glycemic Index rating.

RATATOUILLE

Makes 6 servings as a side dish

1 x 14½oz can no-salt-added tomato puree

1 medium (8oz) eggplant cut into small cubes

2 zucchinis sliced

1 cup onion diced

1 red bell pepper cut into large dice

1 green bell pepper cut into large dice

2 x 14oz cans no-salt-added diced tomatoes

3 tablespoons no-salt-added tomato paste

1 teaspoon crushed garlic (in jar)

1 teaspoon dried basil

2 teaspoons granulated vegetable bouillon (low sodium)

¼ cup hot water

pepper

Place all the ingredients in a large pot. Combine well and bring to boil stirring occasionally. Once boiled reduce heat and place lid on top and cook a further 15 minutes or until vegetables are tender, stirring occasionally. Add pepper to taste.

Suitable to be frozen (but zucchini may go a little soft).

Nutritional Information

PER SERVE	
CALORIES	80
TOTAL FAT	0.5g
SATURATED FAT	0.1g
SODIUM	311mg
CARBS	15.8g
SUGAR	12.9g
FIBER	6.2g
PROTEIN	4.5g
GI RATING	Too low in carbs to score a rating

Dietitian's tip

Lots of vegetables mean lots of vitamins and minerals as well as fiber. A great way to add variety to vegetables. Ideal for people with diabetes and vegetarians.

VEGELICIOUS

Makes 4 servings as a side dish

1 bunch fresh asparagus

cooking spray

1 teaspoon crushed garlic (in jar)

½ cup onion diced

4 cups mushrooms quartered

¼ teaspoon ground turmeric

¼ teaspoon ground cumin

¼ teaspoon ground cilantro

¼ teaspoon ground paprika

1 punnet cherry tomatoes

Cut 1½" off bottom of each asparagus spear and throw away. Cut spears into 1½" pieces. Coat a non-stick frypan with cooking spray, sauté garlic, onion and asparagus for 2 minutes. Add mushrooms and cook for 2 minutes. Add spices and cook for 1 minute. Add tomatoes and cook for 1 to 2 minutes or until heated through.

Not suitable to be frozen.

Nutritional Information

PER SERVE	
CALORIES	46
TOTAL FAT	0.6g
SATURATED FAT	0.1g
SODIUM	16mg
CARBS	5.0g
SUGAR	2.9g
FIBER	4.4g
PROTEIN	5.3g
GI RATING	Too low in carbs to score a rating

Dietitian's tip

Mushrooms contain vitamin B12 responsible for blood cell development. Enjoy this interesting but simple way with vegetables.

VEGETABLE LASAGNE

Makes 6 servings

1 cup each carrots diced, butternut squash diced, celery sliced, small broccoli florets, bell peppers diced and mushrooms sliced

½ cup frozen peas

½ cup frozen corn kernels

1 cup onion diced

1 teaspoon crushed garlic (in jar)

1 x 14½oz can no-salt-added diced tomatoes

1 x 16oz tub low-fat 2% milk cottage cheese

1 tablespoon dried basil

⅓ cup grated parmesan cheese

1 cup no-salt-added tomato paste

cooking spray

8 lasagne sheets

¼ cup extra grated parmesan cheese

Preheat oven to 350°F (180°C) fan forced.

Microwave all vegetables except the mushrooms in a little water on high for 8 minutes then drain. Stir in mushrooms, garlic and diced tomatoes to cooked vegetables. Put mix to one side. In a medium size bowl combine cottage cheese, basil, ⅓ cup parmesan cheese and tomato paste.

Coat a large lasagne dish with cooking spray, spread ⅓ of the vegetable mixture over base. Top with 4 lasagne sheets, spread ½ the vegetable mix on top, cover with ½ the cottage cheese mixture, and repeat this step again. Sprinkle extra parmesan cheese evenly over the top. Cover with aluminum foil (coat foil with cooking spray to stop cheese from sticking). Bake for 35-40 minutes, remove foil and cook a further 5-10 minutes until cheese is golden brown.

Suitable to be frozen.

Nutritional Information

PER SERVE

CALORIES	275
TOTAL FAT	5.7g
SATURATED FAT	2.9g
SODIUM	481mg
CARBS	35.4g
SUGAR	22.4g
FIBER	7.9g
PROTEIN	20.7g
GI RATING	Low

Dietitian's tip

The high protein alternatives and low-fat cheeses make this an ideal dish for vegetarians who have diabetes.

Sides and Light Meals

TACOS

Makes 12 individual servings

Filling

1 x 14½oz can kidney beans

cooking spray

½lb lean ground beef 4% fat

1 teaspoon crushed garlic (in jar)

½ cup onion finely diced

1 x 14½oz can no-salt-added diced tomatoes

4 tablespoons no-salt-added tomato paste

1 teaspoon granulated beef bouillon (low sodium)

2 tablespoons 30% less sodium taco seasoning

Taco

12 taco shells medium size

⅓ cup shredded sharp 2% milk reduced-fat cheese

1½ cups fresh tomatoes chopped

3 cups lettuce finely shredded

Add on extras per taco

1 teaspoon no-fat sour cream

1 teaspoon avocado mashed (add 1.1g fat)

To make filling: Drain and rinse kidney beans. In a non-stick frypan that has been generously coated with cooking spray, sauté ground beef and garlic until browned. Add onion and cook for 2 minutes. Add canned tomatoes, tomato paste, bouillon and taco seasoning stirring well. Fold in kidney beans and simmer for 3 minutes.

To assemble: In each taco shell spoon one twelfth of meat filling, top with 1 teaspoon of cheese, about 2 tablespoons of fresh tomato and ¼ cup of lettuce, repeat this process for each taco shell.

Variations: Replace beef with extra lean 99% fat-free ground turkey.

Taco filling suitable to be frozen.

Nutritional Information

PER SERVE	BEEF	TURKEY
CALORIES	136	132
TOTAL FAT	4.8g	4.3g
SATURATED FAT	1.3g	1.0g
SODIUM	271mg	268mg
CARBS	15.2g	15.2g
SUGAR	4.3g	4.3g
FIBER	3.9g	3.9g
PROTEIN	8.4g	8.8g
GI RATING	Medium	Medium

Dietitian's tip

These tacos are packed with vitamins, minerals and antioxidants. Family members will enjoy being involved in assembling their own meals. A great introduction for children to the art of healthy cooking.

CHILI BEEF

Makes 6 servings

cooking spray

1lb lean ground beef 4% fat

1 teaspoon crushed garlic (in jar)

½ cup onion diced

1 cup green bell peppers diced

1½ cups tomatoes diced

1 cup frozen corn kernels

1 tablespoon granulated beef bouillon (low sodium)

1½ teaspoons ground paprika

1½ teaspoons ground cumin

¼ teaspoon ground chili powder

4 tablespoons no-salt-added tomato paste

1 x 16oz can chili beans

1 x 10¾oz can tomato soup (Healthy Request Campbell's®)

1 cup water

pepper

Coat a non-stick frypan with cooking spray and brown ground beef with garlic for 3 minutes. Add onion, bell peppers, tomatoes and corn and cook until beef and vegetables are cooked through.

Add the bouillon, paprika, cumin, chili powder, tomato paste and chili beans and combine. Finally add canned soup and water and bring to boil. Add pepper to taste. Reduce heat and slow boil for 3 minutes then serve.

Variation: Replace beef with extra lean 99% fat-free ground turkey.

Suitable to be frozen.

Nutritional Information

PER SERVE	BEEF	TURKEY
CALORIES	235	221
TOTAL FAT	4.3g	2.3g
SATURATED FAT	1.6g	0.6g
SODIUM	566mg	556mg
CARBS	28.9g	28.9g
SUGAR	8.9g	8.9g
FIBER	6.8g	6.8g
PROTEIN	22.1g	23.6g
GI RATING	Low	Low

Dietitian's tip

Adding beans means more fiber, which is ideal for general health and wellbeing.

HAM AND CHEESE OMELETTE

Makes 1 serving

¼ cup 98% fat-free ham

3 egg whites

¼ cup shredded sharp 2% milk reduced-fat cheese

cooking spray

Cut ham into strips. In a medium size mixing bowl beat egg whites until stiff peaks form. Using a knife gently fold in cheese and ham. In a heated non-stick frypan coated with cooking spray pour mixture into centre. Cook for 3 minutes on moderate heat (the base will burn otherwise) until golden brown, turn gently and cook a further 3 minutes or until cooked.

Variation: Omit cheese and ham for a plain omelette.

Not suitable to be frozen.

Nutritional Information

PER SERVE	HAM/CHEESE	PLAIN
CALORIES	117	44
TOTAL FAT	4.6g	0g
SATURATED FAT	2.6g	0g
SODIUM	559mg	163mg
CARBS	1.1g	0.4g
SUGAR	0.4g	0.4g
FIBER	0g	0g
PROTEIN	18.6g	10.4g
GI RATING	Too low in carbs to score a rating	

Dietitian's tip

A delicious omelette, serve with low Glycemic Index whole wheat bread.

MEXICAN LAYERED DIP

Makes 16 servings as an appetizer

1 x 16oz can refried beans

1 x 10oz jar chunky tomato salsa (spicy hot)

1 tablespoon 30% less sodium taco seasoning

8oz mashed avocado

1 x 6oz tub non-fat natural yogurt

¼ cup shredded sharp 2% milk reduced-fat cheese

½ cup tomato diced

3 green onions sliced

⅓ cup bell peppers diced

In a medium size mixing bowl combine refried beans and salsa together. Spread over the base of a 9" pie dish. Mix the taco seasoning with avocado and gently spread over top of bean mix.

Spread yogurt over avocado then sprinkle tomato, bell peppers, green onion and cheese over top of yogurt. Refrigerate until required. Serve with rice crackers or reduced fat corn chips.

Not suitable to be frozen.

Nutritional Information

PER SERVE

CALORIES	77
TOTAL FAT	4.2g
SATURATED FAT	1.1g
SODIUM	299mg
CARBS	6.3g
SUGAR	3.1g
FIBER	1.8g
PROTEIN	3.0g
GI RATING	Low

Dietitian's tip

Refried beans are low in fat, high in fiber and have a low Glycemic Index.

PIZZA STRUDEL

Makes 4 servings

1 cup mushrooms chopped

1 cup bell peppers diced

1 cup green onions chopped
or onion diced

½ cup tomato diced

¾ cup 98% fat-free ham diced

1 cup sharp 2% milk reduced-
fat shredded cheese

2 tablespoons grated
parmesan cheese

1 teaspoon crushed garlic (in jar)

½ teaspoon dried basil

8 sheets filo pastry

cooking spray

2 tablespoons no-salt-
added tomato paste

Preheat oven to 400°F (200°C) fan forced.

Mix all ingredients, except filo pastry and tomato paste in a large bowl. Fold out filo pastry sheets, placing one sheet on top of the other, spraying with cooking spray between each layer. Spread tomato paste in centre of filo pastry, spoon pizza filling on top. Spray edges with cooking spray then fold right and left edges inwards, spray again. Roll pastry and filling carefully.

Place strudel with fold side underneath on a flat baking pan that has been coated with cooking spray. Spray top of strudel with cooking spray, pierce top to allow steam to escape. Bake for 35-40 minutes or until golden brown. Serve immediately as pastry will soften when left. To crisp again, either place back in oven or under griller.

Variations: Omit ham for vegetarian strudel and add ½ cup diced celery or add 4 sliced black olives (add 1g fat per person), or replace ham with 4oz raw skinless chicken breast (cook in pan coated with cooking spray) then dice and add to mix.

Suitable to be frozen but you will need to place in oven to crisp pastry once thawed.

Nutritional Information

PER SERVE	PIZZA	VEGETARIAN	CHICKEN
CALORIES	207	194	225
TOTAL FAT	7.1g	6.8g	7.5g
SATURATED FAT	3.6g	3.5g	3.7g
SODIUM	678mg	475mg	477mg
CARBS	22.6g	22.6g	22.6g
SUGAR	3.3g	3.3g	3.3g
FIBER	2.6g	2.9g	2.6g
PROTEIN	14.1g	11.1g	17.6g
GI RATING	Medium	Medium	Medium

Dietitian's tip

To lower the sodium content in this recipe choose the vegetarian or chicken versions.

MEXICAN MEATBALLS
Makes 6 servings

½ cup dried breadcrumbs

½ cup no-fat milk

1¼lb lean ground beef 4% fat

1 envelope 30% less sodium taco seasoning mix

1 small onion finely diced

¼ cup tomato ketchup

½ cup fresh chopped parsley

1 egg white

pepper

cooking spray

Preheat oven to 375°F (190°C) fan forced.

Mix breadcrumbs and milk in a small bowl, leave for 2 minutes.
In a large bowl combine all ingredients. Add pepper to taste. Mix well then roll into 18 small balls.

Place meatballs on a flat baking pan that has been coated with cooking spray. Bake 30-40 minutes or until cooked, turning once. Serve hot or cold.

Variations: Replace ground beef with 99% fat-free (extra lean) ground turkey, or to make meatballs hotter add extra chilli powder to mix, or to add a sauce pour a heated jar of tomato salsa over cooked meatballs.

Suitable to be frozen.

Nutritional Information

PER SERVE	BEEF	TURKEY
CALORIES	179	162
TOTAL FAT	4.1g	1.6g
SATURATED FAT	1.7g	0.5g
SODIUM	429mg	417mg
CARBS	10.9g	10.9g
SUGAR	5.9g	5.9g
FIBER	0.7g	0.7g
PROTEIN	22.4g	24.3g
GI RATING	Medium	Medium

Dietitian's tip
The use of no-fat milk and very lean ground beef makes this a low calorie alternative to traditional meatballs. A great recipe promoting heart health.

TURKEY ROAST WITH CRANBERRY SAUCE

Makes 6 servings

1½ cups light cranberry juice

¼ cup dried cranberries cut in half

1 teaspoon granulated chicken bouillon (low sodium)

1 tablespoon fresh lemon juice

½ teaspoon dijon mustard (in jar)

2 tablespoons cornstarch

1lb cooked lean deli sliced turkey breast

In a small saucepan place all ingredients except turkey. Using a whisk blend together, once boiled reduce to a slow boil for 3 minutes. Leave to one side. Heat turkey in microwave then divide into 6 equal servings. Pour an equal amount of sauce over turkey slices.

Suitable to be frozen.

Nutritional Information

PER SERVE

CALORIES	167
TOTAL FAT	3.2g
SATURATED FAT	0.7g
SODIUM	210mg
CARBS	12.9g
SUGAR	9.9g
FIBER	0.3g
PROTEIN	22.4g
GI RATING	Low

Dietitian's tip

Studies have shown that many people who suffer from bladder infections have fewer episodes when they drink cranberry juice daily.

SYMPLE DAMPER
Makes 10 slices

3 cups self-rising flour
1 teaspoon sugar
½ teaspoon salt
1 egg white
1 x 12oz bottle of beer
cooking spray

Preheat oven to 350°F (180°C) fan forced.

In a large bowl fold all ingredients together using a wooden spoon. Place mixture into a loaf pan that has been coated with cooking spray. Bake for approximately 1 hour. Best eaten that day.

Variations: For garlic damper add 1 teaspoon crushed garlic to ingredients. For herb damper add 1 teaspoon dried mixed herbs to ingredients.

Suitable to be frozen.

Nutritional Information

PER SLICE

CALORIES	157
TOTAL FAT	0.5g
SATURATED FAT	0.1g
SODIUM	397mg
CARBS	30.6g
SUGAR	0.4g
FIBER	1.6g
PROTEIN	4.6g
GI RATING	High

Dietitian's tip

A high Glycemic Index bread. Best to have this with baked beans to lower the Glycemic Index and make it suitable for people with diabetes.

STUFFED POTATOES

Makes 6 servings

6 x 8oz potatoes

For a crispy skin: Preheat oven to 400°F (200°C) fan forced.
Wash potatoes keeping skin on. Bake on middle shelf for 1-1¼ hours or until soft when squeezed.

For a soft skin: Wash potatoes, pierce skin a few times with fork. Place a layer of absorbent paper towel on turntable in microwave. Arrange potatoes around outer edge, cover with paper towel and microwave on high for 5 minutes. Turn potatoes over and cook a further 5 minutes or until soft when squeezed.

Fillings:
Bolognaise Use recipe for Bolognaise on page 151. Spoon mixture into cut potato, sprinkle 2 teaspoons of sharp 2% reduced-fat shredded cheese over filling (optional). Garnish with chopped salad (optional).

Mexican Use recipe for Chilli Beef on page 61. Spoon mixture into cut potato, sprinkle 2 teaspoons of sharp 2% reduced-fat shredded cheese over filling (optional). Garnish with chopped salad (optional).

Sweet Corn and Bacon In a little water microwave 1 cup diced onion and 3 cups frozen corn kernels on high for 5 minutes. Stir in 3 cups canned creamed corn, microwave for 2 minutes. Microwave or dry fry 5oz diced lean Canadian style bacon 95% fat-free, drain on paper towel. Spoon one sixth of corn mixture and one sixth of diced lean bacon into cut potato. Sprinkle 2 teaspoons of sharp 2% reduced-fat shredded cheese over filling (optional). Garnish with chopped salad (optional).

Vegetarian Use recipe for Ratatouille on page 53. For a variation add some sliced carrots, mushrooms and broccoli instead of eggplant. Spoon mixture into cut potato, and if you wish sprinkle 2 teaspoons sharp 2% reduced-fat shredded cheese over filling (optional). Garnish with chopped salad (optional).

Tuna Use recipe for Tomato Tuna Casserole omitting the bread topping on page 94. Sprinkle 2 teaspoons of sharp 2% reduced-fat shredded cheese over filling (optional). Garnish with chopped salad (optional).

All fillings are suitable to be frozen.

NOTE: To know nutritional breakdown for above fillings add the Plain Potato breakdown per serve to the recipe breakdown found on the page of recipe used.

Nutritional Information

PER SERVE	PLAIN POTATO	CORN/BACON
CALORIES	150	370
TOTAL FAT	0.2g	4.9g
SATURATED FAT	0g	1.8g
SODIUM	82mg	398mg
CARBS	30.4g	64.0g
SUGAR	1.1g	11.2g
FIBER	4.6g	9.7g
PROTEIN	5.5g	17.1g
GI RATING	Medium	Medium

Dietitian's tip
A great low fat meal option particularly when topped with salad such as shredded lettuce, diced tomato, bell peppers and cucumber. This makes it a high fiber meal and suitable for bowel health.

TURKEY BURGER
Makes 6 patties

Turkey Patties

1¼lb 99% fat-free extra-lean ground turkey

1 egg white

½ teaspoon crushed garlic (in jar)

½ cup onion finely diced or green onions chopped

½ cup dried breadcrumbs

½ teaspoon dried basil

2 tablespoons sweet chili sauce

cooking spray

Burger Assembly

6 x 2oz whole wheat bread rolls

3 small tomatoes sliced

24 slices cucumber

3 cups lettuce shredded

6 tablespoons 80% less fat mayonnaise (Best Foods®)

To make patties: In a large mixing bowl combine all ingredients and mix well. Shape into 6 patties and place into a non-stick frypan coated with cooking spray. Cook for 3 minutes each side or until cooked.

To assemble burgers: Cut rolls in half, grill until toasted brown. Place salad on base of roll then top with patty and salad. Spread 1 tablespoon of mayonnaise on lid, then place on top of salad.

Variation: Omit the roll and salad and serve with vegetables, mashed potato and gravy.

Patties suitable to be frozen.

Nutritional Information

PER SERVE	BURGER	PATTY ONLY
CALORIES	331	150g
TOTAL FAT	5.9g	1.8g
SATURATED FAT	0.9g	0.5g
SODIUM	662mg	240mg
CARBS	36.1g	8.7g
SUGAR	8.7g	2.0g
FIBER	6.3g	1.0g
PROTEIN	32.6g	23.9g
GI RATING	Medium	Medium

Dietitian's tip
To know if ground turkey or chicken is lean, look for the least amount of white pieces in the mix. If it has a lot of white pieces it means it has skin processed in as well, which makes it very high in fat.

ZUCCHINI SLICE

Makes 6 servings

2 whole eggs

3 egg whites

2 packed cups zucchini grated

2 cups mixed vegetables e.g. carrot grated, bell peppers diced, celery sliced

1 onion diced

½ cup frozen peas

½ cup frozen corn kernels

¾ cup ham 98% fat-free diced

¾ cup self-rising flour

1 cup shredded sharp 2% milk reduced-fat cheese

cooking spray

Preheat oven to 350°F (180°C) fan forced.

In a large bowl beat eggs and whites well, add all other ingredients except the cheese. Add ⅔ of cheese to mixture and combine well. Coat a 9" quiche or lasagne dish with cooking spray. Spoon mixture into dish and level out. Sprinkle remaining cheese on top.

Bake for 35-40 minutes or until golden brown. This dish is even better if made the night before or left to sit for a few hours before serving.

Variation: To make a vegetarian version omit ham and add 1 cup more vegetables of your choice.

Suitable to be frozen.

Nutritional Information

PER SERVE	SLICE	VEGETARIAN
CALORIES	192	185
TOTAL FAT	6.5g	6.3g
SATURATED FAT	3.0g	2.9g
SODIUM	514mg	344mg
CARBS	19.4g	20.0g
SUGAR	3.1g	3.7g
FIBER	3.7g	4.0g
PROTEIN	14.7g	12.5g
GI RATING	Medium	Medium

Dietitian's tip

Lots of vegetables and the use of minimum animal fat make this a cholesterol-lowering recipe.

LEMON FISH

Makes 4 servings

1 tablespoon light
margarine (Promise®)

¼ teaspoon crushed garlic (in jar)

1 tablespoon all purpose flour

½ cup no-fat milk

½ teaspoon granulated chicken
bouillon (low sodium)

1 tablespoon dry white wine

2 tablespoons fresh lemon juice

1 teaspoon fresh cilantro chopped

pepper

4 x 5oz boneless fish fillets

cooking spray

In a non-stick saucepan melt margarine with garlic, add flour and combine. Slowly add in milk, using a whisk to avoid lumps, until boiling. Add bouillon, wine, lemon juice and cilantro. Add pepper to taste. Cook fish fillets in a non-stick frypan that has been generously coated with cooking spray, turning once. Pour sauce over fillets and serve.

Variations: Replace fish fillets with 4 x 5oz skinless chicken breasts or 1lb raw peeled shrimp.

Suitable to be frozen for 2-3 weeks.

Nutritional Information

PER SERVE	FISH	CHICKEN	SHRIMP
CALORIES	179	193	135
TOTAL FAT	4.6g	4.7g	2.1g
SATURATED FAT	1.3g	1.2g	0.4g
SODIUM	164mg	118mg	438mg
CARBS	3.5g	3.5g	3.5g
SUGAR	1.8g	1.8g	1.8g
FIBER	0.1g	0.1g	0.1g
PROTEIN	30.3g	33.4g	24.6g
GI RATING	Too low in carbs to score a rating		

Dietitian's tip

The recommendation is to have three serves of fish per week so we have sufficient essential fatty acids for our heart health.

CRUMBED FISH WITH LIGHT CHEESE SAUCE

Makes 4 servings

1 egg white

2 tablespoons no-fat milk

½ cup dried breadcrumbs

4 x 5oz boneless fish fillets

cooking spray

Cheese Sauce

1 tablespoon light margarine (Promise®)

2 tablespoons all purpose flour

1½ cups no-fat milk

2 tablespoons grated parmesan cheese

1 teaspoon granulated chicken bouillon (low sodium)

½ cup shredded sharp 2% milk reduced-fat cheese

pepper

On a dinner plate beat egg white and milk together. Pour breadcrumbs onto another plate. Dip fish in egg mix then coat fish with breadcrumbs. Leave to one side.

To make sauce: In a medium size saucepan melt margarine, add flour and stir well. Slowly add milk, using a whisk to avoid lumps. Add parmesan, bouillon and shredded cheese and stir continuously. Add pepper to taste. Leave on a very low heat while cooking the fish.

To cook fish: In a large non-stick frypan that has been generously coated with cooking spray, cook fish fillets for 3 minutes. Coat top of fish generously with cooking spray, then turn and cook a further 3 minutes or until fish is cooked through. Place on serving plates and pour cheese sauce over top.

Fish suitable to be frozen but the cheese sauce is only suitable to be frozen for 2-3 weeks.

Nutritional Information

PER SERVE	
CALORIES	276
TOTAL FAT	7.8g
SATURATED FAT	3.7g
SODIUM	428mg
CARBS	13.4g
SUGAR	5.8g
FIBER	0.5g
PROTEIN	39.6g
GI RATING	Low

Dietitian's tip
Fish has loads of protein and is low in calories and fat. The cheese sauce will help contribute to your calcium intake helping you maintain healthy bones.

FISH ALASKA

Makes 4 servings

1 tablespoon light
margarine (Promise®)

1 heaped tablespoon
all purpose flour

½ cup no-fat milk

¼ cup white wine

½ cup green onions sliced

1 tablespoon fresh chopped parsley

1 x 6oz can crabmeat

pepper

4 x 4oz firm boneless fish fillets

cooking spray

¾ cup shredded sharp 2%
milk reduced-fat cheese

To make sauce: Melt margarine in medium size saucepan, stir in flour with a whisk. Slowly add milk to saucepan, stirring constantly to avoid lumps. Add wine, green onion, parsley and drained crabmeat, mix well. Add pepper to taste.

To cook fish: Cook fish fillets in a non-stick frypan that has been generously coated with cooking spray turning once. Once cooked place fish on a flat baking pan that has been coated with cooking spray then spoon sauce evenly over each fillet. Sprinkle cheese equally over each piece of fish. Grill until golden brown.

Suitable to be frozen.

Nutritional Information	
PER SERVE	
CALORIES	236
TOTAL FAT	8.6g
SATURATED FAT	3.7g
SODIUM	467mg
CARBS	4.0g
SUGAR	1.8g
FIBER	0.2g
PROTEIN	33.8g
GI RATING	Too low in carbs to score a rating

Dietitian's tip

Seafood contains vitamin B1 Thiamine, required for muscle strength, memory and appetite.

GARLIC SHRIMP

Makes 4 servings

cooking spray

1lb raw peeled shrimp

2 teaspoons crushed garlic (in jar)

½ cup green onions sliced

¼ cup white wine

2 tablespoons cornstarch

1 x 12½oz can low-fat
2% evaporated milk

pepper

Coat non-stick frypan with cooking spray then sauté shrimp for 3 minutes. Add garlic, green onions and wine to pan and cook 4-5 minutes. Combine cornstarch with evaporated milk, add to pan, stirring constantly until sauce boils and thickens. Add pepper to taste.

Suitable to be frozen for 2-3 weeks.

Nutritional Information

PER SERVE	
CALORIES	203
TOTAL FAT	0.8g
SATURATED FAT	0.1g
SODIUM	532mg
CARBS	15.8g
SUGAR	12.2g
FIBER	0.4g
PROTEIN	29.4g
GI RATING	Low

Dietitian's tip
This recipe contains shrimp which are naturally high in sodium and cholesterol. It would be advisable that people with diabetes only have this dish occasionally.

SALMON BAKE

Makes 6 servings

1 whole egg

2 egg whites

1 cup no-fat milk

1 x 14½oz can pink salmon
(drained & mashed)

½ cup onion finely diced

½ cup frozen corn kernels

½ cup red bell peppers diced small

3 tablespoons fresh
chopped parsley

½ teaspoon dried dill

1 tablespoon lemon juice

2 cups cooked macaroni pasta

¾ cup shredded sharp 2%
milk reduced-fat cheese

cooking spray

Preheat oven to 350°F (180°C) fan forced.

In a large mixing bowl beat egg, egg whites and milk together. Add all other ingredients except the pasta and cheese, mix well. Fold in the cooked pasta and ⅔ of the cheese, combine together.

Pour mixture into a 9" quiche or pie dish that has been coated with cooking spray. Sprinkle remaining cheese over top. Bake for 45 minutes or until browned and cooked in center. Can be served either hot or cold.

Suitable to be frozen.

Nutritional Information	
PER SERVE	
CALORIES	205
TOTAL FAT	7.4g
SATURATED FAT	3.0g
SODIUM	462mg
CARBS	15.3g
SUGAR	3.5g
FIBER	1.4g
PROTEIN	20.3g
GI RATING	Low

Dietitian's tip

An easy way to help get your recommended three fish serves a week.

TUNA PATTIES
Makes 6 servings

¾lb potatoes

2 x 12oz cans tuna in water

1 cup dried breadcrumbs

1 x 14oz can diced tomato
with capsicum & onion

2 teaspoons granulated chicken
bouillon (low sodium)

3 tablespoons sweet chili sauce

cooking spray

Peel and dice potatoes then microwave on high with a little water for 5-6 minutes or until cooked. Drain well then mash, leave to cool. Drain tuna and break up pieces so they are not too large. Drain canned tomatoes (liquid is not required).

Place all ingredients into a large mixing bowl and combine well using your hands to blend mixture together. Make 12 patties, refrigerate until required. In a large non-stick frypan generously coated with cooking spray, fry patties until browned. Before turning spray tops of patties then carefully turn and cook until browned.

Suitable to be frozen.

Nutritional Information	
PER SERVE	
CALORIES	209
TOTAL FAT	2.8g
SATURATED FAT	0.7g
SODIUM	428mg
CARBS	28.5g
SUGAR	3.5g
FIBER	1.8g
PROTEIN	17.6g
GI RATING	High

Dietitian's tip
Tuna in water provides less sodium than tuna in brine and less fat than tuna in oil. It is a healthy low-calorie option for people with high blood pressure wanting to shed those extra pounds.

OYSTERS ALASKA

Makes 4 servings

1 tablespoon light margarine (Promise®)

1 heaped tablespoon all purpose flour

½ cup no-fat milk

¼ cup white wine

½ cup green onions chopped

1 tablespoon fresh chopped parsley

1 x 6oz can crab meat drained

pepper

4 x 1 dozen natural oysters in shell

1 cup shredded sharp 2% milk reduced-fat cheese

Melt margarine in a medium size saucepan, stir in flour with a whisk. Slowly add milk to saucepan, stirring constantly to avoid lumps. Add wine, green onion, parsley and crab meat, mix well. Add pepper to taste. Place oysters on a flat baking pan. Spoon sauce evenly over each oyster and top with a little cheese. Grill until golden brown.

Not suitable to be frozen.

Nutritional Information	
PER SERVE	
CALORIES	185
TOTAL FAT	9.0g
SATURATED FAT	4.4g
SODIUM	696mg
CARBS	5.2g
SUGAR	2.3g
FIBER	0.4g
PROTEIN	19.8g
GI RATING	Too low in carbs to score a rating

Dietitian's tip

Oysters are high in sodium so reduce to having a half dozen per serve and have as an occasional treat for people with diabetes or high blood pressure.

TUNA TOMATO CASSEROLE

Makes 4 servings

cooking spray

1 teaspoon crushed garlic (in jar)

¾ cup onion diced

¾ cup green bell peppers diced

1 cup carrots cut in half then thinly sliced

1 cup celery sliced

1 x 12oz can tuna in spring water

1 x 6oz can tuna in spring water

2 teaspoons granulated vegetable or chicken bouillon (low sodium)

1 teaspoon dried dill

3 tablespoons no-salt-added tomato paste

1 x 10¾oz can tomato soup (Healthy Request Campbell's®)

½ cup water

Bread Top

3oz whole wheat long bread roll

1 teaspoon crushed garlic (in jar)

1 tablespoon light margarine (Promise®)

1 tablespoon grated parmesan cheese

ground paprika

In a large non-stick saucepan that has been coated with cooking spray, sauté garlic, onion, bell peppers, carrots and celery for 5 minutes. Drain tuna and break up pieces so that they are not too large, add to pan. Mix in bouillon, dill, tomato paste, soup undiluted and water stirring well. Bring to boil then reduce to a slow boil for 3 minutes or until vegetables are cooked to your liking.

To make bread top: Cut bread into twelve slices. In a small bowl combine garlic and margarine then spread evenly over the bread slices. Sprinkle parmesan cheese over top. Sprinkle a light coating of paprika over each slice. Place under griller until top is toasted. Place three slices on top of each serve.

Suitable to be frozen.

Nutritional Information

PER SERVE	WITH BREAD	NO BREAD
CALORIES	295	209
TOTAL FAT	7.2g	3.8g
SATURATED FAT	2.6g	1.4g
SODIUM	627mg	444mg
CARBS	27.2g	17.6g
SUGAR	13.0g	11.4g
FIBER	4.5g	2.8g
PROTEIN	31.2g	26.7g
GI RATING	Medium	Medium

Dietitian's tip

Tuna is naturally low in saturated fat when compared to other protein foods and provides omega-3 fatty acids. It is an excellent food for people with diabetes and heart disease.

Chicken

MARINATED CHICKEN DRUMSTICKS

Makes 6 servings

12 raw chicken drumsticks skin removed (ask your butcher to remove if you don't know how to do this)

Marinade

½ cup soy sauce (low sodium)

½ cup white wine

3 tablespoons no-salt-added tomato paste

½ teaspoon dried tarragon

½ teaspoon dried basil

1 teaspoon crushed garlic (in jar)

1 teaspoon crushed ginger (in jar)

1 teaspoon granulated chicken bouillon (low sodium)

⅓ cup warmed honey

To make marinade: Mix all marinade ingredients together in a medium size bowl. Place drumsticks into a flat container that has a secure lid. Pour marinade over drumsticks, cover and refrigerate overnight to get full flavour. If time doesn't permit allow at least 4 hours. Turn drumsticks occasionally.

Preheat oven to 375°F (190°C) fan forced.
Remove chicken from marinade and place on a baking tray that has been coated with cooking spray. Spoon a little marinade over chicken. Bake for 25-35 minutes or until drumsticks are cooked. Serve hot or cold.

Variations: Replace chicken with lean veal or lean beef steaks.

Suitable to be frozen.

Nutritional Information

PER SERVE

CALORIES	254
TOTAL FAT	10.4g
SATURATED FAT	3.0g
SODIUM	478mg
CARBS	8.4g
SUGAR	7.6g
FIBER	0.2g
PROTEIN	31.8g
GI RATING	Too low in carbs to score a rating

Dietitian's tip

To make this suitable for people with diabetes use a little less soy sauce to reduce the sodium content.

CHICKEN & CORN PIE

Makes 6 servings

Base

½ cup uncooked Basmati rice (or 2 cups cooked)

½ cup onion diced

cooking spray

1 teaspoon each ground cumin, turmeric and cilantro

¼ teaspoon ground chili powder (or to taste)

½ cup dried breadcrumbs

1 egg

1 tablespoon no-fat milk

Filling

2 whole eggs

3 egg whites

½ cup no-fat milk

2 cups zucchini grated

1 x 11oz can creamed corn

1 cup frozen corn kernels

1 cup (about 5 oz) skinless cooked chicken breast shredded

½ cup shredded sharp 2% milk reduced-fat cheese

⅓ cup fresh chopped parsley

½ teaspoon dried tarragon

1 teaspoon granulated chicken bouillon (low sodium)

pepper

¼ cup shredded sharp 2% milk reduced-fat cheese

To make base: Cook rice as described on back of packet. Rinse and drain well. Preheat oven to 375°F (200°C) fan forced. In a non-stick frypan that has been coated with cooking spray sauté onion for 2-3 minutes. Add cumin, turmeric, cilantro and chili powder to pan and cook a further 1 minute. Tip onion mix into a medium size mixing bowl, add in cooked rice and breadcrumbs, and mix well. Beat egg with milk then pour into rice mixture, combine ingredients together well. Coat a 9" pie dish with cooking spray then press rice mixture into dish evenly.

To make filling: In a large mixing bowl beat eggs, egg whites and milk together. Add remaining ingredients except ¼ cup shredded cheese (to put on top of pie), mix all ingredients together well. Add pepper to taste. Pour mixture over rice base, sprinkle remaining cheese over top and bake uncovered for 50-60 minutes or until set and brown on top. Let stand for 10-15 minutes before serving. Serve hot or cold.

Variations: Replace chicken with 1 cup of 98% fat free ham diced or replace chicken with 1 cup drained tuna in water.

Not suitable to be frozen.

Nutritional Information

PER SERVE	CHICKEN	HAM	TUNA
CALORIES	297	271	291
TOTAL FAT	8.0g	7.0g	7.5g
SATURATED FAT	3.0g	2.8g	3.0g
SODIUM	422mg	599mg	430mg
CARBS	36.7g	36.7g	36.7g
SUGAR	6.3g	6.3g	6.3g
FIBER	4.2g	4.2g	4.2g
PROTEIN	21.0g	16.5g	20.5g
GI RATING	Low	Low	Low

Dietitian's tip

Unlike many pies this is low in saturated fat and contains lean meats making it suitable for people with diabetes.

CHICKEN PIZZIOLA

Makes 4 servings

4 x 4oz skinless chicken breasts

½ cup ham 98% fat-free diced

½ cup mushrooms thinly sliced

½ cup bell peppers thinly sliced

½ cup green onions chopped or onion thinly sliced

½ cup tomato diced

1 teaspoon crushed garlic (in jar)

½ teaspoon dried basil

cooking spray

4 dessertspoons no-salt-added tomato paste

1 cup shredded sharp 2% milk reduced-fat cheese

Preheat oven to 350°F (180°C) fan forced.

Flatten chicken breast with meat mallet. In a medium size mixing bowl mix together ham, mushrooms, bell peppers, green onion, tomato, garlic and basil. On a baking tray that has been coated with cooking spray place raw flattened chicken then spread 1 dessertspoon of tomato paste over each breast.

Spread pizza topping evenly over each breast. Sprinkle ¼ cup of cheese over each piece. Bake for 30-40 minutes or until chicken is cooked and topping is golden brown.

Variations: Replace chicken with lean beef steak or turkey breast cutlets extra lean.

Suitable to be frozen.

Nutritional Information

PER SERVE	CHICKEN	BEEF	TURKEY
CALORIES	222	242	217
TOTAL FAT	7.8g	9.5g	6.7g
SATURATED FAT	3.6g	4.5g	3.4g
SODIUM	441mg	449mg	455mg
CARBS	3.5g	3.5g	3.5g
SUGAR	2.5g	2.5g	2.5g
FIBER	1.4g	1.4g	1.4g
PROTEIN	35.1g	34.5g	35.5g
GI RATING	Too low in carbs to score a rating		

Dietitian's tip

This recipe is high in lean protein required for the growth and repair of our cells throughout our lives.

CHICKEN WITH PEPPER SAUCE

Makes 6 servings

1 tablespoon dried medley peppercorn mix

cooking spray

½ cup onion finely chopped

2 teaspoons granulated chicken bouillon (low sodium)

2 tablespoons brandy

¼ cup red wine

2 tablespoons cornstarch

½ cup water

1 x 12½oz can low-fat 2% evaporated milk

pepper

6 x 5oz skinless chicken breasts

Crush peppercorns using a rolling pin. Coat a non-stick saucepan with cooking spray, cook onion and crushed peppercorns 2 minutes, stirring continuously. Add bouillon, brandy, red wine and bring to boil. Combine cornstarch with water, add to pot and bring to boil. Pour in milk, stir ingredients together well. Add pepper to taste.

Once boiled reduce to a low simmer. Cook chicken breasts by grilling, dry bake or pan fry in a non-stick frypan that has been coated with cooking spray. Spoon pepper sauce over chicken and serve.

Variations: Replace chicken with lean beef steak or turkey breast cutlets (extra lean).

Suitable to be frozen for 2-3 weeks.

Nutritional Information

PER SERVE	CHICKEN	BEEF	TURKEY
CALORIES	241	265	234
TOTAL FAT	4.4g	6.5g	2.9g
SATURATED FAT	0.9g	2.0g	0.6g
SODIUM	159mg	169mg	176mg
CARBS	9.4g	9.4g	9.4g
SUGAR	6.7g	6.7g	6.7g
FIBER	0.4g	0.4g	0.4g
PROTEIN	36.3g	35.6g	36.9g
GI RATING	Low	Low	Low

Dietitian's tip

This creamy sauce is surprisingly low in fat due to Annette's clever use of evaporated low-fat milk. People with diabetes who are interested in weight loss will find this recipe delicious.

CRUNCHY NUT CHICKEN

Makes 4 servings

4 x 4oz raw skinless chicken breasts

2 cups corn flakes

⅓ cup macadamia nuts finely chopped

1 teaspoon granulated chicken bouillon (low sodium)

1 egg white

¼ cup no-fat milk

cooking spray

Preheat oven to 350°F (180°C) fan forced.

Flatten chicken breasts with a meat mallet or rolling pin. Place corn flakes in a plastic bag then using a rolling pin or mallet crush finely. Add nuts and bouillon granules into bag and shake, tip onto a flat plate. Using a fork beat egg white and milk together.

Pour onto a plate and coat chicken in egg mixture. Then place into crumb mixture and coat each side of chicken well. Place on a flat baking pan that has been coated with cooking spray, spray chicken with cooking spray and bake 25-30 minutes or until cooked and coating is golden brown.

Variation: For an even lower fat count omit macadamia nuts and add ½ cup more corn flakes to crumbs.

Not suitable to be frozen.

Nutritional Information

PER SERVE	MACADAMIA	WITHOUT NUTS
CALORIES	291	207
TOTAL FAT	11.8g	2.9g
SATURATED FAT	2.0g	0.8g
SODIUM	313mg	312mg
CARBS	17.6g	17.0g
SUGAR	3.1g	2.6g
FIBER	1.3g	0.6g
PROTEIN	29.3g	28.4g
GI RATING	High	High

Dietitian's tip

Macadamia nuts add a great taste to this recipe and provide lots of mono and polyunsaturated fats that are needed for a healthy heart.

HOMESTEAD CHICKEN PIE

Makes 6 servings

Pie Filling

1¼lb raw skinless chicken breasts

cooking spray

1 cup onion diced

½lb mushrooms quartered

1 cup no-fat milk

1 x 10¾oz can cream of mushroom soup (Healthy Request Campbell's®)

1 teaspoon granulated chicken bouillon (low sodium)

2 tablespoons fresh chopped parsley

pepper

Pie Top

1 tablespoon light margarine (Promise®)

¼ cup no-fat milk

1 egg white

1 cup self-rising flour

pinch of salt

Preheat oven 450°F (220°C) fan forced.

To make pie filling: Cut chicken into bite size pieces. Coat a large non-stick frypan with cooking spray, sauté chicken for 3 minutes. Add onion and cook for 2 minutes. Add mushrooms and cook for 2 minutes. Combine milk with soup and bouillon then pour into pan. Stir in parsley. Add pepper to taste. Once mixture has boiled pour into a casserole dish. Leave to one side.

To make pie top: Melt margarine in microwave, add to milk and combine. Add egg white and beat with a fork until blended. Place flour and salt into a medium size mixing bowl, pour milk mixture into flour and combine. You may need to use your hands to combine mixture, but don't over knead the dough as it will make it tough. Turn onto a floured surface and roll out dough to the size of the casserole dish. Using a rolling pin, roll up pie top and lift onto top of filling.

Trim edges and make a decorative edge by using the back of a fork, or pinch the edges with the tips of your fingers. Using a pastry brush, brush a little milk over top. Bake for 10 minutes or until top is golden and cooked in the centre.

Variations: Replace chicken with very lean beef steak or lean lamb steaks or firm tofu.

Suitable to be frozen for 2-3 weeks.

Nutritional Information

PER SERVE	CHICKEN	BEEF	LAMB	TOFU
CALORIES	256	272	265	230
TOTAL FAT	4.4g	5.9g	5.6g	7.9g
SATURATED FAT	1.1g	1.8g	2.0g	0.5g
SODIUM	501mg	508mg	523mg	455mg
CARBS	24.9g	24.9g	24.9g	28.6g
SUGAR	4.4g	4.4g	4.4g	5.4g
FIBER	2.7g	2.7g	2.7g	2.7g
PROTEIN	28.6g	28.2g	28.0g	16.7g
GI RATING	Medium	Medium	Medium	Medium

Dietitian's tip

Unlike most pies this is low in saturated fat and contains lean meat. I would highly recommend this for people with diabetes.

MANGO CHICKEN

Makes 6 servings

cooking spray

½ cup onion diced

1 teaspoon crushed garlic (in jar)

1½lbs raw skinless chicken breasts cut into strips

1 teaspoon curry powder

2 tablespoons no-salt-added tomato paste

2 teaspoons granulated chicken bouillon (low sodium)

2 tablespoons cornstarch

1½ cups mango nectar

1 x 12½oz can low-fat 2% evaporated milk

1 teaspoon imitation coconut extract

1 x 15oz can mango slices in natural juice drained

In a non-stick frypan that has been coated with cooking spray sauté onion and garlic for 2 minutes. Add chicken and sauté for 5 minutes or until nearly cooked. Combine curry powder, tomato paste and bouillon with chicken, cook for 1 minute.

Blend cornstarch with mango nectar, add to pan. Add milk and coconut extract to pan and stir continuously until sauce boils. Add drained mango slices then serve with boiled rice or pasta. Don't over boil the sauce as the milk may separate.

Variation: Replace canned mango slices with fresh mango flesh or for Apricot Chicken replace mango nectar and canned fruit with apricot nectar and canned apricot halves (in natural juice).

Suitable to be frozen for 2-3 weeks.

Nutritional Information

PER SERVE

CALORIES	251
TOTAL FAT	3.9g
SATURATED FAT	0.7g
SODIUM	148mg
CARBS	23.5g
SUGAR	20.5g
FIBER	0.8g
PROTEIN	30.8g
GI RATING	Low

Dietitian's tip
The mango in this recipe provides the carbohydrates for this meal. People with diabetes may like to include a green vegetable with this meal rather than another source of carbohydrates.

INDIAN BUTTER CHICKEN
Makes 6 servings

1¾lbs skinless chicken breasts

cooking spray

1 cup onion diced

1 teaspoon crushed garlic (in jar)

½ teaspoon crushed ginger (in jar)

1 teaspoon ground cilantro

1 teaspoon ground turmeric

1 teaspoon ground coriander

2 teaspoons ground paprika

½ teaspoon ground cumin

⅛ teaspoon chili powder

2 teaspoons granulated chicken bouillon (low sodium)

4 tablespoons no-salt-added tomato paste

1 x 12½oz can low-fat 2% evaporated milk

Cut chicken into bite sized pieces. Coat a large non-stick frypan or wok with cooking spray, sauté chicken, onion, garlic and ginger until chicken pieces are nearly cooked. Add all the spices and bouillon. Combine with chicken for 1 minute. Add tomato paste and fold through chicken. Add milk to pan and combine with ingredients. Once boiled serve.

Variations: Replace chicken with lean beef steak, lean pork steak or tofu.

Suitable to be frozen for 2-3 weeks.

Nutritional Information

PER SERVE	CHICKEN	BEEF	PORK	TOFU
CALORIES	216	239	208	181
TOTAL FAT	4.4g	6.4g	3.5g	9.4g
SATURATED FAT	0.8g	1.9g	0.7g	0.1g
SODIUM	159mg	168mg	172mg	94mg
CARBS	9.7g	9.7g	9.7g	15.2g
SUGAR	7.8g	7.8g	7.8g	9.2g
FIBER	0.3g	0.3g	0.3g	0.3g
PROTEIN	34.9g	34.2g	34.9g	18.3g
GI RATING	Too low in carbs to score a rating			

Dietitian's tip
This recipe is traditionally very high in fat. As this recipe does not contain butter but uses cooking oil it has a much lower saturated fat and calorie count, making it an ideal food choice.

MEXICAN CHICKEN STACK
Makes 6 servings

cooking spray

1 cup uncooked basmati rice

1 tablespoon granulated chicken bouillon (low sodium)

2½ cups boiling water

1 x 16oz can chili beans (Bush Best®)

1½ teaspoons cajun seasoning

1½ teaspoons ground cumin

1lb raw skinless chicken breasts

1 cup bell peppers finely diced

1 cup celery finely diced

1 cup onion finely diced

1 cup broccoli very small florets

1 cup cauliflower very small florets

1 teaspoon crushed garlic (in jar)

1 x 14½oz can no-salt-added tomato puree

½ cup shredded sharp 2% milk reduced-fat cheese

LAYER 1: In a large saucepan (that has a lid), generously coat base with cooking spray, sauté rice and bouillon for 1 minute. Add boiling water, once boiling put lid on and reduce to a slow boil for 15 minutes. Do not remove lid whilst cooking. Remove from heat and give it a good stir, leave to one side.

LAYER 2: Using a food processor or stick blender puree chili beans until a smooth consistency is formed.

LAYER 3: Mix cajun seasoning and cumin together, coat chicken. In a non-stick frypan that has been generously coated with cooking spray, cook chicken breasts. Cut into small dice then leave to one side.

LAYER 4: Cook vegetables in a microwave dish with a little water on high for 4 minutes, drain.

LAYER 5: Combine garlic with tomato puree, leave to one side.

To assemble stack: Divide cooked rice equally in the centre of 6 dinner plates making a round shape the size of a side plate. Spread an equal amount of bean mix over top of rice then top with chopped chicken. Place vegetables over chicken then pour tomato puree over top. Sprinkle shredded cheese evenly over puree. Microwave each plate for 3-4 minutes or until mixture has heated through all layers.

Variations: Replace chicken with turkey breast cutlets extra lean or lean beef steak.

Not suitable to be frozen.

Nutritional Information

PER SERVE	CHICKEN	TURKEY	BEEF
CALORIES	242	238	255
TOTAL FAT	4.4g	3.7g	5.6g
SATURATED FAT	1.8g	1.6g	2.4g
SODIUM	478mg	487mg	483mg
CARBS	27.7g	27.7g	27.7g
SUGAR	5.5g	5.5g	5.5g
FIBER	6.8g	6.8g	6.8g
PROTEIN	26.2g	26.5g	25.8g
GI RATING	Low	Low	Low

Dietitian's tip
Beans are packed with soluble fiber, which slows down the stomach emptying, therefore helping people to feel full for longer after eating. An excellent choice for people with diabetes.

STUFFED APRICOT CHICKEN

Makes 4 servings

Stuffing

1 cup cooked basmati rice

½ cup dried apricots small dice

1 teaspoon granulated chicken bouillon (low sodium)

¼ cup green onions sliced

3 tablespoons Pad Thai sauce (in jar)

2 teaspoons Thai red curry paste (in jar)

4 x 4oz raw skinless chicken breasts

toothpicks

cooking spray

Apricot sauce

½ teaspoon crushed ginger (in jar)

¼ cup brandy

1 cup apricot nectar

1 teaspoon granulated chicken bouillon (low sodium)

2 teaspoons cornstarch

¼ cup water

Preheat oven to 350°F (180°C) fan forced.

To make stuffing: Combine rice, apricots, bouillon, green onions and both Thai sauce and paste together. Using a sharp knife, make a pocket lengthways inside each chicken breast (don't cut all the way through). Use your finger to widen and open the hole to allow for filling.

Spoon ¼ of the mixture into each breast pocket and push filling deep into breast. Seal opening with toothpicks. Place chicken onto a flat baking pan that has been generously coated with cooking spray. Spray over top of chicken. Bake for 25-30 minutes or until chicken is cooked through.

To make sauce: In a small saucepan that has been coated with cooking spray, sauté ginger for 15 seconds, add brandy. Using a whisk stir in apricot nectar and bouillon. Blend cornstarch with water and whisk into pot, bring to boil. Pour ¼ of sauce over top of each chicken breast.

Variation: For Stuffed Mango Chicken replace dried apricots with dried mango and apricot nectar with mango nectar.

Suitable to be frozen.

Nutritional Information

PER SERVE	
CALORIES	319
TOTAL FAT	3.6g
SATURATED FAT	1.0g
SODIUM	351mg
CARBS	34.7g
SUGAR	20.4g
FIBER	2.5g
PROTEIN	28.3g
GI RATING	Low

Dietitian's tip

Basmati rice has a lower Glycemic Index than other varieties, making it a suitable choice for people with diabetes or who are interested in good health.

BEEF STROGANOFF

Makes 4 servings

cooking spray

1 teaspoon crushed garlic (in jar)

1lb lean beef steak cut into strips

1 cup onion sliced

3 cups mushrooms sliced

2 gherkins finely chopped

2 teaspoons granulated beef bouillon (low sodium)

2 tablespoons no-salt-added tomato paste

1 tablespoon ground paprika

1 tablespoon cornstarch

1 x 12½oz can low-fat 2% evaporated milk

pepper

Coat a large non-stick frypan with cooking spray, add garlic and beef strips, toss together until browned. Add onion to pan and cook for 2 minutes, place mushrooms into pan and cook a further 2 minutes.

Add gherkins, bouillon, tomato paste, paprika and stir well. Blend cornstarch into milk, add to pan stirring continuously until sauce boils. Add pepper to taste.

Variations: Replace beef with skinless chicken breast or turkey breast cutlets (extra lean) or lean veal steaks.

Suitable to be frozen for 2-3 weeks.

Nutritional Information

PER SERVE	BEEF	CHICKEN	TURKEY	VEAL
CALORIES	259	239	234	230
TOTAL FAT	4.8g	3.1g	1.9g	2.1g
SATURATED FAT	1.6g	0.7g	0.5g	0.5g
SODIUM	302mg	294mg	308mg	335mg
CARBS	18.7g	18.7g	18.7g	18.7g
SUGAR	15.5g	15.5g	15.5g	15.5g
FIBER	2.3g	2.3g	2.3g	2.3g
PROTEIN	33.8g	34.4g	34.8g	34.0g
GI RATING	Low	Low	Low	Low

Dietitian's tip
Stroganoff is normally high in saturated fat. In the variations Annette uses very lean meat, skinless chicken, turkey and veal which reduce the amount of saturated fats in this recipe, which makes it suitable for people with diabetes.

LASAGNE

Makes 8 servings

Meat Sauce

1½lbs lean ground beef 4% fat

cooking spray

2 x 14½oz cans no-salt-added tomato puree

4½oz can no-salt-added tomato paste

1 cup water

1 onion finely diced

2 teaspoons crushed garlic (in jar)

1 tablespoon granulated beef bouillon (low sodium)

2 teaspoons dried oregano

pepper

White Sauce

1 tablespoon light margarine (Promise®)

3 tablespoons all purpose flour

2½ cups no-fat milk

pepper

8 instant lasagne sheets

¾ cup shredded sharp 2% milk reduced-fat cheese

To make meat sauce: Brown meat in a large saucepan that has been coated with cooking spray, drain well and remove to a plate. In same saucepan add all other ingredients, bring to boil, simmer 5 minutes. Return meat to pan, add pepper to taste then cook a further 5 minutes. Leave meat sauce to one side.

To make white sauce: Melt margarine in a medium size saucepan, add flour, and mix well with a whisk to avoid lumps. Slowly add milk, stir constantly until sauce boils, add pepper to taste. Remove from heat, leave for a few minutes to allow sauce to thicken.

Preheat oven to 350°F (180°C) fan forced.

To assemble lasagne Spoon one third of meat sauce over base of a large lasagne dish, cover with half of white sauce. Top with 4 lasagne sheets. Spread half of meat sauce over lasagne, cover with remaining white sauce, top with remaining lasagne sheets. Spread with remainder of meat sauce and sprinkle with cheese.

Cover with aluminum foil (coat with cooking spray to stop cheese sticking). Bake 40-45 minutes, remove foil, cook a further 5-10 minutes until pasta is cooked and cheese is golden brown.

Suitable to be frozen.

Nutritional Information

PER SERVE

CALORIES	278
TOTAL FAT	7.2g
SATURATED FAT	3.2g
SODIUM	242mg
CARBS	26.7g
SUGAR	10.5g
FIBER	3.4g
PROTEIN	27.7g
GI RATING	Low

Dietitian's tip

At last a lasagne that is low in saturated fat, low in calories and has moderate sodium. Great for those aiming to manage their blood pressure and diabetes.

BEEF STEAK PIE

Makes 4 servings

1½lbs lean braising beef steak diced

cooking spray

1 cup onion cut into large dice

1½ cups water

2 tablespoons Worcestershire sauce

1 tablespoon granulated beef bouillon (low sodium)

3 tablespoons all purpose flour

7 sheets filo pastry

To make filling: Brown beef in non-stick saucepan that has been coated with cooking spray. Drain liquid, add onion stirring together for 3 minutes. Add 1¼ cups of water (leaving remaining ¼ cup to blend with flour later), add Worcestershire sauce and bouillon, bring to the boil and then reduce to a simmer for 30 minutes with lid on. Stir occasionally. Blend flour with remaining water and stir into pan, boil for 2-3 minutes or until sauce thickens. Leave filling to cool.

Preheat oven to 400°F (200°C) fan forced.

To assemble pie: Spray a 9" pie dish with cooking spray. Cut filo sheets in half (use 8 for base, 6 for top). Layer the pie dish with 8 cut sheets, in a rotating fashion, spraying with cooking spray between each sheet. Spoon meat mixture on top of pastry. Place remaining filo sheets by layering over top of filling in a rotating fashion, spraying with cooking spray between sheets. Crinkle edges together, spray with cooking spray. Bake for 30-35 minutes or until golden brown. Serve immediately as pastry will soften when left. To crisp again either place back in oven or under griller.

Variation: For Steak and Kidney Pie replace 8oz of stewing beef steak with 8oz kidney diced (equalling 1lb stewing beef steak and ½lb kidneys)

Suitable to be frozen but you will need to place in the oven to crisp pastry once thawed.

Nutritional Information

PER SERVE	BEEF	BEEF/KIDNEY
CALORIES	255	245
TOTAL FAT	5.2g	4.7g
SATURATED FAT	1.9g	1.7g
SODIUM	379mg	426mg
CARBS	24.9g	24.9g
SUGAR	2.0g	2.0g
FIBER	1.1g	1.1g
PROTEIN	28.2g	26.6g
GI RATING	Medium	Medium

Dietitian's tip

Filo pastry is low in fat and makes a great pie. Using filo and Annette's lean meat pie filling gives people with diabetes a healthy pie option.

MACARONI BEEF

Makes 6 servings

Meat Sauce

cooking spray

1lb lean ground beef 4% fat

¾ cup carrot grated

¾ cup zucchini grated

½ cup onion finely diced

½ cup frozen peas

1 x 10¾oz can tomato soup
(Healthy Request Campbell's®)

1 tablespoon granulated beef
bouillon (low sodium)

4 tablespoons no-salt-
added tomato paste

3 cups cooked macaroni pasta

Topping

1 tablespoon light
margarine (Promise®)

3 tablespoons all purpose flour

1½ cups no-fat milk

¾ cup shredded sharp 2%
milk reduced-fat cheese

Preheat oven to 350°F (180°C) fan forced.

To make meat sauce: Cook beef in a large non-stick saucepan that has been coated with cooking spray. Drain liquid then return meat to pan. Add in carrots, zucchini, onion, peas and soup, cook for 2 minutes stirring continuously. Add bouillon and tomato paste and cook a further 5 minutes stirring frequently. Fold in cooked macaroni pasta and mix together well. Pour mixture into a lasagne dish.

To make topping: Melt margarine in saucepan, add flour, and cook for 1 minute. Slowly add milk using a whisk to avoid lumps, stir continuously until boiling. Pour sauce over the meat, sprinkle with shredded cheese. Bake for 25-30 minutes or until top is golden brown.

Variation: Omit topping.

Suitable to be frozen.

Nutritional Information		
PER SERVE	WITH TOPPING	WITHOUT
CALORIES	331	243
TOTAL FAT	8.2g	4.2g
SATURATED FAT	3.6g	1.6g
SODIUM	482mg	326mg
CARBS	37.2g	29.5g
SUGAR	10.3g	7.1g
FIBER	4.0g	3.8g
PROTEIN	27.2g	21.4g
GI RATING	Low	Low

Dietitian's tip
The carbohydrate in the pasta is absorbed slowly into the body. This will give insulin ample time to take the sugar out of the blood and into the cells.

MILD SWEET CURRY

Makes 6 servings

1 cup each of sliced carrots, onion and celery

½ cup red bell pepper sliced

½ cup green bell pepper sliced

1 cup quartered small yellow squash (4-5 whole)

1½ cups water

cooking spray

1¼lb very lean beef steak diced

2 teaspoons crushed ginger (in jar)

1 teaspoon ground cilantro

1 teaspoon ground cumin

1 teaspoon ground turmeric

1 teaspoon ground sweet paprika

¼ teaspoon ground chili powder (or to taste)

2 teaspoons granulated beef bouillon (low sodium)

½ cup raisins

1 cup peeled apple diced

1 teaspoon imitation coconut extract

1 x 12½oz can low-fat 2% evaporated milk

½ cup no-fat milk

2 tablespoons cornstarch

Microwave vegetables on high for 8 minutes with 1½ cups of water. Coat a non-stick frypan with cooking spray, brown beef for 5 minutes, drain excess liquid, add ginger to beef, cook a further 1 minute. Combine cilantro, cumin, turmeric, paprika and chili powder with meat, cook for 1 minute.

Drain vegetables but keep 1 cup of stock water aside. Dissolve bouillon in stock water, add to frypan with raisins and diced apple, cook a further 2 minutes. Add vegetables, reduce heat, cover and simmer for 5 minutes. Blend coconut extract, evaporated milk, no-fat milk and cornstarch together, then stir into pan. Heat until mixture thickens.

Variations: Replace beef with very lean lamb or skinless chicken breast.

Suitable to be frozen for 2-3 weeks.

Nutritional Information

PER SERVE	BEEF	LAMB	CHICKEN
CALORIES	254	246	238
TOTAL FAT	4.9g	4.7g	3.5g
SATURATED FAT	1.4g	1.6g	0.6g
SODIUM	180mg	195mg	173mg
CARBS	24.4g	24.4g	24.4g
SUGAR	21.1g	21.1g	21.1g
FIBER	3.0g	3.0g	3.0g
PROTEIN	27.4g	27.2g	27.9g
GI RATING	Low	Low	Low

Dietitian's tip

Annette's clever use of coconut extract and evaporated milk gives the flavour without the saturated fat making this a healthy heart choice.

SHEPHERD'S PIE

Makes 8 servings

Meat sauce

1 cup onion diced

1 cup carrot diced

1 cup zucchini diced

1 cup celery sliced

1 cup small broccoli florets

1 cup small cauliflower florets

½ cup frozen peas

½ cup frozen corn kernels

½ cup frozen or fresh
green bean slices

1¼lbs lean ground beef 4% fat

cooking spray

1½ tablespoons granulated
beef bouillon (low sodium)

1½ packets (about 9 teaspoons)
brown gravy mix (French's®)

3 tablespoons tomato ketchup

3 tablespoons Worcestershire sauce

2 tablespoons oyster sauce

2½ cups water

1 tablespoon cornstarch

Potato top

2¼lbs potatoes

¼ cup no-fat milk

¾ cup shredded sharp 2%
milk reduced-fat cheese

To make meat sauce: Microwave all the vegetables in a little water on high for 10 minutes. Cook ground beef in large saucepan or boiler that has been coated with cooking spray. Once cooked through add bouillon, gravy mix powder, tomato ketchup, Worcestershire and oyster sauce. Combine with meat then add 2 cups of the water and combine well.

Once boiled add in the pre-cooked drained vegetables then put lid on and simmer for 5 minutes, stirring occasionally (be careful that mixture does not stick to base of pot). Blend cornstarch with the ½ cup of remaining water then add to pan and combine well with mixture. Leave to one side.

To make potato top: Peel and dice potatoes. Microwave in a little water until cooked (about 12-15 minutes). Once cooked drain then mash with no-fat milk. Re-heat meat sauce then pour into a large lasagne dish.

Using a spoon and fork put small dobs of mashed potato over top of the meat; run a fork over top to spread potato evenly. Sprinkle with grated cheese and place dish under the griller until potato has browned on top.

Suitable to be frozen.

Nutritional Information

PER SERVE	
CALORIES	272
TOTAL FAT	5.8g
SATURATED FAT	2.6g
SODIUM	698mg
CARBS	30.9g
SUGAR	6.7g
FIBER	5.2g
PROTEIN	23.8g
GI RATING	High

Dietitian's tip

The potato provides ample carbohydrates for people with diabetes. To make this a complete meal add green vegetables on the side.

STEAK DIANE

Makes 6 servings

cooking spray

2 teaspoons crushed garlic (in jar)

1 cup green onions sliced

2 tablespoons brandy

½ cup red wine

1 tablespoon granulated beef bouillon (low sodium)

2 tablespoons Worcestershire sauce

2 tablespoons cornstarch

½ cup water

1 x 12½oz can low-fat 2% evaporated milk

½ cup no-fat milk

pepper

6 x 5oz flattened lean beef steaks

Coat a non-stick saucepan with cooking spray, cook garlic and green onions for 2 minutes stirring continuously. Add brandy, red wine, bouillon and Worcestershire sauce, bring to boil and simmer for 3 minutes stirring occasionally.

Mix cornstarch with water, add to pot and bring to boil, stir ingredients well. Add evaporated and no-fat milk and combine then add pepper to taste. Bring back to boil, reduce to a low simmer.

To cook steak, grill or panfry to preferred liking e.g. rare, medium or well done. Spoon Diane sauce equally over each cooked steak and serve.

Variations: Replace steak with skinless chicken breast or turkey breast cutlets extra lean.

Sauce suitable to be frozen for 2-3 weeks.

Nutritional Information

PER SERVE	BEEF	CHICKEN	TURKEY
CALORIES	291	266	260
TOTAL FAT	6.7g	4.5g	3.1g
SATURATED FAT	2.1g	0.9g	0.6g
SODIUM	277mg	267mg	283mg
CARBS	13.1g	13.1g	13.1g
SUGAR	8.9g	8.9g	8.9g
FIBER	0.4g	0.4g	0.4g
PROTEIN	36.6g	37.3g	37.9g
GI RATING	Low	Low	Low

Dietitian's tip

The clever use of evaporated and no-fat milk instead of cream makes this sauce lower in fat making it suitable for people with diabetes.

RIPPA RISSOLES (beef patties)

Makes 6 servings

½ cup uncooked brown rice

¾ cup carrots grated

¾ cup zucchini grated

1 small onion finely diced

1¼lb lean ground beef 4% fat

2 teaspoons granulated beef bouillon (low sodium)

2 tablespoons oyster sauce

1 envelope spring vegetable Cup-a-soup (Lipton®)

1 egg white

pepper

cooking spray

Follow cooking instructions on rice packet. Rinse and drain well. Place vegetables in a large mixing bowl. Add all remaining ingredients including cooked rice to bowl and combine well. Use your hands to achieve a good consistency with mixing patties. Add pepper to taste. Shape into 12 patties. If time permits refrigerate patties for a few hours before cooking.

Generously coat a large non-stick frypan with cooking spray, fry patties 3-5 minutes on each side or until cooked through and browned on both sides.

Variations: Replace beef with either very lean ground chicken or turkey extra lean 99% fat free.

Suitable to be frozen.

Nutritional Information

PER SERVE	BEEF	CHICKEN	TURKEY
CALORIES	205	201	188
TOTAL FAT	4.5g	4.7g	2.0g
SATURATED FAT	1.7g	1.2g	0.5g
SODIUM	406mg	401mg	393mg
CARBS	17.4g	17.4g	17.4g
SUGAR	3.2g	3.2g	3.2g
FIBER	1.7g	1.7g	1.7g
PROTEIN	22.8g	22.6g	24.7g
GI RATING	High	High	High

Dietitian's tip

Adding rice and vegetables to patties will lower the total fat and provide dietary fiber required for normal bowel function.

STICKY PORK CHOPS

Makes 4 servings

⅓ cup plum sauce (in jar)

2 teaspoons sweet chili sauce

1 tablespoon soy sauce
(low sodium)

2 tablespoons honey

cooking spray

4 x 7oz lean mid loin pork chops

½ teaspoon crushed garlic (in jar)

½ teaspoon crushed ginger (in jar)

⅛ teaspoon ground Chinese 5 spice

In a small bowl combine plum, sweet chili, soy sauce and honey. Coat a large non-stick frypan with cooking spray, fry pork chops until cooked to your liking. Remove chops onto a large dinner plate, leave to one side.

Re-spray frypan with cooking spray and sauté garlic and ginger for 1 minute. Pour in honey mixture and add Chinese 5 spice, mixing well. Once sauce boils simmer for 2 minutes. Return chops to pan to reheat and coat with sauce.

Variations: Replace pork with 4 x 5oz skinless chicken breasts or 4 x 5oz lean beef steaks or 14oz firm tofu cut into 4 slices.

Suitable to be frozen.

Nutritional Information				
PER SERVE	PORK	CHICKEN	BEEF	TOFU
CALORIES	298	241	265	167
TOTAL FAT	3.4g	3.3g	5.4g	6.0g
SATURATED FAT	1.2g	0.8g	2.0g	0.1g
SODIUM	439mg	374mg	384mg	302mg
CARBS	10.4g	10.4g	10.4g	14.4g
SUGAR	8.9g	8.9g	8.9g	9.9g
FIBER	0.1g	0.1g	0.1g	0.1g
PROTEIN	46.2g	32.4g	31.7g	10.4g
GI RATING	Low	Low	Low	Low

Dietitian's tip

The honey adds flavour and small quantities can be included in the eating plan for people with diabetes.

CHICKEN CASHEW STIR FRY

Makes 4 servings

¼ cup raw cashew nuts

cooking spray

1lb skinless chicken breast sliced

1 teaspoon crushed garlic (in jar)

½ cup onion sliced

½ small fresh red chili
sliced (optional)

½ cup green bell peppers
cut into strips

½ cup red bell peppers
cut into strips

16 snow peas cut in half

½ cup carrots cut in half
then in thin slices

½ cup green onions sliced

1 teaspoon granulated chicken
bouillon (low sodium)

2 teaspoons fish sauce

2 teaspoons oyster sauce

2 teaspoons soy sauce (low sodium)

1 pinch of sugar

1 pinch of pepper

1 tablespoon cornstarch

1 cup water

Place a sheet of aluminum foil over a flat baking tray. Spread cashews over baking tray then place under grill until browned (be careful as they burn quickly), leave to one side.

Heat wok or large non-stick frypan and coat with cooking spray, sauté chicken and garlic together until cooked. Place chicken into a bowl and leave to one side. Spray pan again with cooking spray then add the onion, chili, bell peppers, snow peas and carrots, stir 3-5 minutes. Add green onions, bouillon, sauces, sugar, pepper and mix together.

Blend cornstarch with water and pour into pan, stir well. Add chicken back to pan and cook for 2-3 minutes more. Once sauce has thickened serve with basmati rice or noodles. Sprinkle cashews over each serve.

Variation: Omit cashews for a lower fat count.

Suitable to be frozen.

Nutritional Information		
PER SERVE	WITH CASHEWS	WITHOUT
CALORIES	203	160
TOTAL FAT	6.7g	3.0g
SATURATED FAT	1.4g	0.7g
SODIUM	544mg	543mg
CARBS	8.0g	6.7g
SUGAR	5.0g	4.5g
FIBER	2.1g	1.7g
PROTEIN	28.9g	27.6g
GI RATING	Too low in carbs to score a rating	

Dietitian's tip

Cashew nuts add variety to stir fry dishes and are a great source of unsaturated fat making this recipe a healthy heart choice.

BEEF STIR FRY

Makes 4 servings

cooking spray

1 teaspoon crushed ginger (in jar)

1 teaspoon crushed garlic (in jar)

1lb lean beef steak cut into strips

1 cup red bell peppers sliced

1 cup small broccoli florets

1 cup snow peas

1 cup mushrooms sliced

1 cup bok choy coarsely sliced

½ cup green onions sliced

2 tablespoons white wine

1 tablespoon soy sauce
(low sodium)

2 tablespoons hoisin sauce

1 dessertspoon sugar

1 tablespoon cornstarch

1 teaspoon granulated beef
bouillon (low sodium)

¾ cup water

Sauté ginger and garlic for 1 minute in non-stick frypan that has been coated with cooking spray. Add beef strips and sauté until cooked. Drain and set aside. In same frypan spray again, stir fry bell peppers and broccoli for 3 minutes then add in remaining vegetables, toss until tender crisp. Stir in wine, soy sauce, hoisin sauce and sugar into pan.

Combine cornstarch, bouillon and water together then add to pan, bring to boil mixing well. Add cooked steak back to pan and combine with ingredients. Once meat is heated through serve with basmati rice or noodles.

Variations: Replace beef with skinless chicken breast.
Replace hoisin and soy sauce with ¾ cup plum sauce.
Replace hoisin sauce with oyster sauce.
For a vegetarian stir fry omit meat and replace with vegetable bouillon and add 1 cup celery sliced, 1 cup carrots sliced and 1 cup bean shoots, or replace steak with 14oz firm tofu cut into strips.

Suitable to be frozen.

Nutritional Information

PER SERVE	BEEF	CHICKEN	VEGETABLE	TOFU
CALORIES	200	181	72	139
TOTAL FAT	4.9g	3.1g	0.5g	6.4g
SATURATED FAT	1.6g	0.7g	0.1g	0.1g
SODIUM	237mg	228mg	210mg	172mg
CARBS	7.6g	7.6g	10.6g	11.6g
SUGAR	4.7g	4.7g	7.0g	5.7g
FIBER	3.1g	3.1g	5.6g	3.1g
PROTEIN	29.3g	29.8g	5.7g	14.2g
GI RATING	Too low in carbs to score a rating			

Dietitian's tip

It is recommended that lean red meat be eaten three times a week providing iron for oxygen transport throughout the body.

CHINESE OMELETTE

Makes 2 servings

Omelette

3 egg whites

2 whole eggs

½ teaspoon granulated beef bouillon (low sodium)

cooking spray

¼ cup green onions sliced

½ cup mushrooms sliced

¼ cup frozen peas

1½ cups bean shoots

Sauce

1 teaspoon cornstarch

2 teaspoons oyster sauce

⅓ cup water

To make omelette: Using a whisk, beat egg whites, whole eggs and bouillon together in a bowl. In a medium size non-stick frypan that has been generously coated with cooking spray, sauté green onion, mushrooms, peas and bean shoots for 2 minutes.

Spread vegetables out evenly in the pan, pour egg mix over the top. Cook until egg mixture has browned on bottom, (it should still be runny on top), don't have the heat too hot or it will burn bottom of omelette. Place frypan under a heated griller until omelette is cooked on top. Cut in half and carefully lift omelette onto plates.

To make sauce: Combine cornstarch and oyster sauce with water then pour into pan, stir well until boiled. Pour sauce over omelette.

Variations: For a chicken omelette - in a small non-stick frypan that has been generously coated with cooking spray, fry 2oz raw skinless chicken breast until cooked, shred. For a shrimp omelette - add 2oz cooked peeled shrimp, cut in half.

Not suitable to be frozen.

Nutritional Information

PER SERVE	PLAIN	CHICKEN	SHRIMP
CALORIES	143	177	173
TOTAL FAT	5.5g	7.1g	5.8g
SATURATED FAT	1.6g	2.1g	1.7g
SODIUM	403mg	419mg	525mg
CARBS	7.8g	7.8g	7.8g
SUGAR	3.0g	3.0g	3.0g
FIBER	4.0g	4.0g	4.0g
PROTEIN	16.3g	23.1g	22.8g
GI RATING	Too low in carbs to score a rating		

Dietitian's tip

It is recommended that we have at least 5 serves of vegetables a day. This omelette provides an ideal way to include vegetables in a healthy eating plan for people with diabetes and heart disease.

FRIED RICE

Makes 8 servings as a side dish

2 cups uncooked basmati rice

1 whole egg

1 egg white

¼ cup no-fat milk

cooking spray

¾ cup Canadian style bacon
95% fat-free diced

¾ cup green onions sliced

⅓ cup frozen peas

2oz cooked peeled shrimp

3 tablespoons soy sauce
(low sodium)

Cook rice as instructed on back of rice packet. Once cooked rinse and drain well. Spread out on a flat tray and leave to dry for at least 1 hour. In a small bowl beat egg and egg white with milk. Coat a non-stick frypan with cooking spray and cook bacon, remove and leave to one side.

Re-spray frypan and cook egg mix like an omelette. Once cooked remove from pan and cut into strips. Re-spray frypan again and add cooked rice, green onions, peas, shrimp, cooked bacon and egg mix, combine well. Pour in soy sauce and stir through mixture. Cook 2-3 minutes, stirring frequently.

Suitable to be frozen.

Nutritional Information

PER SERVE	
CALORIES	222
TOTAL FAT	1.5g
SATURATED FAT	0.5g
SODIUM	383mg
CARBS	42.2g
SUGAR	1.1g
FIBER	1.6g
PROTEIN	9.4g
GI RATING	Medium

Dietitian's tip
Basmati rice has a lower Glycemic Index than other varieties of rice, making it an excellent choice for people with diabetes or anyone interested in good health.

ORIENTAL PORK

Makes 4 servings

1lb lean pork steaks

cooking spray

2 teaspoons crushed ginger (in jar)

1 cup celery sliced

1 cup fresh green beans sliced

1 cup onion sliced

¾ cup fresh baby corn cut in half

1 cup bell peppers sliced

2 teaspoons granulated chicken bouillon (low sodium)

1 tablespoon soy sauce (low sodium)

1 teaspoon fish sauce

2 teaspoons sweet chili sauce

2 tablespoons crunchy peanut butter

1 tablespoon cornstarch

1 x 12½oz can low-fat 2% evaporated milk

½ teaspoon imitation coconut extract

Cut pork into thin strips. Coat a large non-stick frypan or wok with cooking spray, sauté pork and ginger until browned. Add celery, beans, onion, corn and bell peppers and cook for 4 to 5 minutes or until vegetables are cooked to your liking. Add bouillon, soy, fish and sweet chili sauces and peanut butter to pan, blending well. In a small mixing bowl combine cornstarch with evaporated milk and coconut extract, then pour into pan, stir continuously until boiling. Serve with basmati rice or noodles.

Variations: Replace pork with lean beef steak or skinless chicken breasts or 14oz firm tofu. To reduce the sodium count replace crunchy peanut butter with low sodium crunchy peanut butter.

Suitable to be frozen for 2-3 weeks.

Nutritional Information

PER SERVE	PORK	BEEF	CHICKEN	TOFU
CALORIES	320	347	328	285
TOTAL FAT	7.9g	10.4g	8.7g	12.1g
SATURATED FAT	1.4g	2.4g	1.5g	0.9g
SODIUM	625mg	622mg	614mg	557mg
CARBS	26.0g	26.0g	26.0g	30.0g
SUGAR	15.5g	15.5g	15.5g	16.5g
FIBER	3.3g	3.3g	3.3g	3.3g
PROTEIN	37.4g	36.9g	37.4g	21.8g
GI RATING	Too low in carbs to score a rating			

Dietitian's tip

Lean pork is low in fat and high in B vitamins required for normal cell function.

SATAY PORK BURGER

Makes 6 servings

Satay Sauce

2½ tablespoons peanut butter

½ cup 80% less fat mayonnaise (Best Foods®)

1 teaspoon Thai red curry paste

1½ teaspoons soy sauce (low salt)

Meat Patties

1¼lb very lean ground pork

1 egg white

2 teaspoons granulated beef bouillon (low sodium)

1 teaspoon crushed garlic (in jar)

1 teaspoon crushed ginger (in jar)

1 teaspoon Thai red curry paste

2 teaspoons lemon grass (in jar) sliced

cooking spray

Burger Assembly

6 x 2oz whole wheat bread rolls

3 small tomatoes sliced

24 slices cucumber

3 cups lettuce shredded

To make satay sauce: In a small mixing bowl combine satay sauce ingredients mixing well.

To make meat patties: In a large mixing bowl place ground pork, egg white, bouillon, garlic, ginger, Thai red curry paste and lemon grass. Use your hands to combine mixture well. Divide into 6 round shaped patties. In a large non-stick frypan that has been generously coated with cooking spray, fry patties until cooked on both sides.

To assemble burgers: Cut rolls in half, grill until toasted brown. Place salad on base of bread roll then top with meat patty and one sixth of satay sauce, place lid on top.

Variations: Omit bread roll and salad and instead have patties with sauce served with potato and vegetables or mixed salad. Or replace ground pork with lean ground chicken or lean ground beef 4% fat.

Meat patties and sauce are suitable to be frozen.

Nutritional Information

PER SERVE	PORK	CHICKEN	BEEF	PATTY/SAUCE
CALORIES	336	351	355	178
TOTAL FAT	10.4g	12.9g	12.7g	8.3g
SATURATED FAT	1.6g	2.3g	2.7g	1.2g
SODIUM	676mg	682mg	687mg	377mg
CARBS	29.9g	29.9g	29.9g	3.9g
SUGAR	7.8g	7.8g	7.8g	2.4g
FIBER	5.8g	5.8g	5.8g	0.5g
PROTEIN	32.4g	30.6g	30.9g	23.8g
GI RATING	Medium	Medium	Medium	Medium

Dietitian's tip
Peanuts are high in protein and mono and polyunsaturated fats and low in saturated fat (18%). These qualities make it a great food for people with diabetes and heart disease.

SPICY THAI FISH

Makes 4 servings

1lb boneless fish fillets

1 onion

cooking spray

1 teaspoon crushed garlic (in jar)

1 teaspoon crushed ginger (in jar)

1 cup bell peppers diced

1 cup celery sliced

1 cup carrot sliced

1 cup snow peas cut in half

1 x 14¾oz can no-salt-added crushed tomatoes

2 tablespoons no-salt-added tomato paste

1 tablespoon fresh cilantro chopped

2 teaspoons lemon grass chopped (in jar)

4 teaspoons Thai red curry paste

1 teaspoon granulated chicken or vegetable bouillon (low sodium)

⅛ teaspoon ground chili powder (optional)

2 teaspoons fish sauce

1 tablespoon cornstarch

¾ cup water

Use a firm-fleshed fish in this recipe to avoid fish breaking up or crumbling. Cut fish into bite size pieces. Peel and cut onion in half then slice. Generously coat a non-stick frypan or wok with cooking spray, sauté garlic and ginger for 30 seconds, add fish pieces to pan and toss gently together until fish is just cooked (about 2 to 3 minutes). Remove fish from pan, leave to one side.

Re-spray pan with cooking spray and sauté onion, bell peppers, celery and carrots for 3 minutes. Add snow peas and cook for 2 minutes, stirring frequently to avoid vegetables burning. Place tomatoes, tomato paste, cilantro, lemon grass, red curry paste, bouillon, chili powder and fish sauce into pan and mix well.

Combine cornstarch into water and add to pan, stir until thickened. Gently fold fish through sauce (to avoid it breaking up). Once fish is heated through serve with basmati rice or noodles.

Variations: Replace fish with either skinless chicken breasts cut into strips or 14oz firm tofu diced.

Suitable to be frozen.

Nutritional Information

PER SERVE	FISH	CHICKEN	TOFU
CALORIES	194	206	163
TOTAL FAT	3.4g	3.5g	6.9g
SATURATED FAT	0.9g	0.8g	0.1g
SODIUM	461mg	424mg	368mg
CARBS	13.9g	14.0g	17.9g
SUGAR	9.1g	9.1g	10.1g
FIBER	3.8g	3.8g	3.8g
PROTEIN	26.6g	29.1g	13.5g
GI RATING	Low	Low	Low

Dietitian's tip

A very low fat interesting recipe. The basmati rice will increase the carbohydrate content. For most people ½ to ¾ of a cup of cooked basmati rice is sufficient.

Sauces for pasta

TUSCANY SAUCE

Makes 4 servings

cooking spray

1 teaspoon crushed garlic (in jar)

¾ cup onion diced

1 cup bell peppers diced

1 cup celery diced

1 cup zucchini diced

1 cup mushrooms sliced

1 x 14½oz can no-salt-added tomato puree

1 x 14½oz can no-salt-added diced tomatoes

2 tablespoons no-salt-added tomato paste

1 teaspoon dried basil

2 teaspoons granulated vegetable bouillon (low salt)

pepper

In a large saucepan coated with cooking spray sauté garlic and vegetables for 3 minutes stirring frequently. Add all other ingredients and simmer for 10 minutes, stirring occasionally. Add pepper to taste. Serve sauce over pasta.

Variations: Add ¾lb skinless chicken breasts diced or add ¾lb lean beef steak diced or add ¾lb firm tofu diced. Sauté meat or tofu in pan with garlic until cooked then remove onto a plate. Cook the vegetables and make Tuscany Sauce as per the recipe. Once sauce is ready add meat back to pan and serve with pasta.

Suitable to be frozen.

Nutritional Information

PER SERVE	TUSCANY	CHICKEN	BEEF	TOFU
CALORIES	87	182	197	159
TOTAL FAT	0.6g	2.5g	3.8g	5.7g
SATURATED FAT	0.1g	0.6g	1.2g	0.1g
SODIUM	104mg	151mg	157mg	109mg
CARBS	17.0g	17.0g	17.0g	20.4g
SUGAR	11.9g	11.9g	11.9g	12.8g
FIBER	5.6g	5.6g	5.6g	5.6g
PROTEIN	4.9g	24.2g	23.8g	13.4g
GI RATING	Low	Low	Low	Low

Dietitian's tip

Packed with a variety of vegetables, this dish provides important vitamins and minerals.

BOLOGNAISE SAUCE

Makes 4 servings

cooking spray

1lb lean ground beef 4% fat

1 x 14½oz can no-salt-added tomato puree

¼ cup no-salt-added tomato paste

1 teaspoon crushed garlic (in jar)

½ cup onion diced

1 teaspoon dried oregano

1 teaspoon granulated beef bouillon (low sodium)

1 cup water

pepper

Brown beef in a large saucepan that has been coated with cooking spray, drain well, remove to plate. Using the same saucepan mix tomato puree, tomato paste, garlic, onion, oregano, bouillon and water together. Add pepper to taste.

Bring to boil, reduce heat and simmer for 5 minutes covered. Add ground beef back to the pot and simmer for 5 minutes. Serve with spaghetti.

Suitable to be frozen.

Nutritional Information

PER SERVE	
CALORIES	177
TOTAL FAT	4.8g
SATURATED FAT	2.0g
SODIUM	151mg
CARBS	8.2g
SUGAR	5.8g
FIBER	2.7g
PROTEIN	25.7g
GI RATING	Low

Dietitian's tip

Buying the 4% fat ground beef makes it suitable to include in meals for people with diabetes.

BOSCAIOLA SAUCE

Makes 4 servings

4oz Canadian style bacon 95% fat free

cooking spray

1 cup onion finely diced

1 cup bell peppers diced

1 teaspoon crushed garlic (in jar)

2 cups mushrooms sliced

1 tablespoon no-salt-added tomato paste

2 teaspoons granulated beef bouillon (low sodium)

⅛ teaspoon ground chili powder (or to taste)

1 x 12½oz can low-fat 2% evaporated milk

1 tablespoon cornstarch

½ cup no-fat milk

pepper

Dice bacon. In a non-stick saucepan coated with cooking spray sauté bacon until browned. Add onion, bell peppers, and garlic, cook 2 minutes. Add mushrooms and cook 2 minutes. Add tomato paste, bouillon and chili powder. Pour in evaporated milk and stir ingredients together.

Now combine cornstarch with no-fat milk then add to pot. Bring to boil then add pepper to taste and serve over pasta.

Variation: For a vegetarian version replace bacon with a can of drained and washed kidney beans and swap beef bouillon for vegetable bouillon granules.

Suitable to be frozen for 2-3 weeks.

Nutritional Information

PER SERVE	BACON	VEGETARIAN
CALORIES	149	169
TOTAL FAT	3.1g	2.2g
SATURATED FAT	0.6g	0.2g
SODIUM	486mg	363
CARBS	15.7g	24.3g
SUGAR	12.9g	14.5g
FIBER	1.8g	6.0g
PROTEIN	15.0g	13.7g
GI RATING	Low	Low

Dietitian's tip

When choosing bacon, look for the leanest available and trim all visible fat to help keep saturated fat to a minimum.

CHICKEN PESTO SAUCE

Makes 6 servings

Pesto Paste

2 teaspoons pine nuts

½ teaspoon crushed garlic (in jar)

2 teaspoons grated parmesan cheese

2 tablespoons water

½ teaspoon granulated chicken bouillon (low sodium)

½ bunch fresh basil leaves

1 teaspoon virgin olive oil

Sauce

1lb raw skinless chicken breasts

cooking spray

2 teaspoons crushed garlic (in jar)

½ cup onion diced

2 cups mushrooms sliced

4 tablespoons no-salt-added tomato paste

2 teaspoons granulated chicken bouillon (low sodium)

2 tablespoons cornstarch

¾ cup no-fat milk

1 x 12½oz can low-fat 2% evaporated milk

pepper

To make pesto: Spread a sheet of aluminum foil over a flat baking tray and spread pine nuts on top. Place under grill and brown pine nuts but be careful as they can burn easily. Process pine nuts and garlic in a food processor for 1 minute. Add parmesan cheese, water, granulated bouillon and basil leaves, process for a further 2 minutes or until finely chopped. Add olive oil and process for 1 more minute. Leave to one side.

To make sauce: Cut chicken breasts into strips. In a large non-stick frypan that has been coated generously with cooking spray, sauté garlic and chicken until browned. Add onion and cook 2 minutes. Toss in mushrooms and cook a further 2 minutes. Add tomato paste, bouillon and pesto paste and mix well. Combine cornstarch with no-fat milk, pour into pan with evaporated milk and bring to boil. Add pepper to taste. Fold cooked pasta into sauce until heated through, then serve.

Variations: Replace chicken with 1lb lean beef steak, turkey breast cutlets extra lean or raw peeled shrimp.

Suitable to be frozen for 2-3 weeks.

Nutritional Information

PER SERVE	CHICKEN	BEEF	TURKEY	SHRIMP
CALORIES	189	202	185	171
TOTAL FAT	4.0g	5.1g	3.2g	2.7g
SATURATED FAT	0.9g	1.5g	0.7g	0.5g
SODIUM	167mg	172mg	176mg	390mg
CARBS	14.0g	14.0g	14.0g	14.0g
SUGAR	11.6g	11.6g	11.6g	11.6g
FIBER	1.4g	1.4g	1.4g	1.4g
PROTEIN	24.4g	24.1g	24.7g	22.8g
GI RATING	Low	Low	Low	Low

Dietitian's tip

Pasta is a low Glycemic Index carbohydrate food. However it is still important that people with diabetes moderate their serving sizes to minimize the possibility of blood sugars going up and down.

CARBONARA SAUCE

Makes 6 servings

cooking spray

1 teaspoon crushed garlic (in jar)

¾ cup onion diced

1 cup 98% fat-free ham diced

3 cups mushrooms sliced

1 tablespoon light margarine (Promise®)

2 tablespoons all purpose flour

1 x 12½oz can low-fat 2% evaporated milk

½ cup no-fat milk

1 x 10¾oz can cream of mushroom soup (Healthy Request Campbell's®)

1 teaspoon granulated beef bouillon (low sodium)

2 tablespoons grated parmesan cheese

pepper

Coat a large non-stick saucepan with cooking spray. Sauté garlic and onion for 2 minutes, toss in ham and cook 2 minutes. Add sliced mushrooms and cook a further 2-3 minutes. Remove from pan and set to one side.

In same saucepan melt margarine, add flour, mixing well. Slowly add in evaporated milk and then no-fat milk, mixing continually using a whisk until smooth. Stir in soup undiluted, beef bouillon and parmesan cheese. Return mushroom mixture to pot, combine well. Add pepper to taste. Pour sauce over pasta and serve.

Suitable to be frozen for 2-3 weeks.

Nutritional Information	
PER SERVE	
CALORIES	143
TOTAL FAT	4.1g
SATURATED FAT	1.1g
SODIUM	572mg
CARBS	14.9g
SUGAR	8.6g
FIBER	1.7g
PROTEIN	11.5g
GI RATING	Low

Dietitian's tip

98% fat-free ham can be used in all recipes to lower the amount of saturated fat and make it suitable for people with diabetes.

SEAFOOD MARINARA SAUCE

Makes 4 servings

1 teaspoon crushed garlic (in jar)

cooking spray

1lb seafood marinara mix

½ cup green onions sliced or onion chopped

½ cup white wine

1 x 14½oz can no-salt-added diced tomatoes

2 teaspoons no-salt-added tomato paste

2 heaped tablespoons cornstarch

¾ cup low-fat 2% evaporated milk

Sauté garlic in a non-stick frypan that has been coated with cooking spray for 1 minute then add seafood, green onions and wine to pan, cook for 3 minutes. Add canned tomatoes and tomato paste then cook for a further 3 minutes. Combine cornstarch with milk, add to pan stirring well, bring to boil then pour over cooked pasta.

Note: Marinara mix is a combination of raw seafood such as fish, shrimp, calamari, octopus and mussels.

Variation: Replace marinara mix with 1lb peeled raw shrimp.

Suitable to be frozen for 2-3 weeks.

Nutritional Information		
PER SERVE	MARINARA	SHRIMP
CALORIES	198	223
TOTAL FAT	1.5g	1.6g
SATURATED FAT	0.1g	0.2g
SODIUM	564mg	590mg
CARBS	23.9g	14.7g
SUGAR	9.1g	8.4g
FIBER	1.9g	1.9g
PROTEIN	16.9g	32.0g
GI RATING	Low	Low

Dietitian's tip

The health benefits of eating fish are many. This recipe is a great way to enjoy seafood in a delicious tasting sauce.

MEDITERRANEAN SAUCE

Makes 4 servings

cooking spray

1 cup onion diced

1 teaspoon crushed garlic (in jar)

1 x 14½oz can no-salt-added diced tomatoes

¼ cup Spanish black olives sliced

⅓ cup sundried tomatoes sliced

1 teaspoon dried basil

1 teaspoon granulated vegetable bouillon (low sodium)

1 tablespoon cornstarch

1 cup low-fat 2% evaporated milk

In a non-stick saucepan that has been coated with cooking spray sauté onion and garlic for 2 minutes. Add all other remaining ingredients except milk and cornstarch and stir together. Once mixture has boiled blend cornstarch with milk then add to pan and combine ingredients. Stir continuously until mixture returns to boil then serve over pasta.

Suitable to be frozen for 2-3 weeks.

Nutritional Information	
PER SERVE	
CALORIES	131
TOTAL FAT	4.4g
SATURATED FAT	0.1g
SODIUM	194mg
CARBS	16.7g
SUGAR	10.6g
FIBER	1.7g
PROTEIN	6.4g
GI RATING	Low

Dietitian's tip

A scrumptious sauce to serve with pasta. Pasta is a great basis to meals as it has a low Glycemic Index.

LITE PESTO

Makes ⅔ cup or 24 teaspoons

1 heaped tablespoon pine nuts

1 teaspoon crushed garlic (in jar)

1 tablespoon grated parmesan cheese

¼ cup water

1 teaspoon granulated vegetable bouillon (low sodium)

1 bunch fresh basil (3oz leaves only)

2 teaspoons virgin olive oil

Spread a sheet of aluminum foil over a flat baking tray and spread pine nuts on top. Place under grill and brown pine nuts but be careful as they can burn easily. Process pine nuts and garlic for 1 minute in a food processor. Add parmesan cheese, water, granulated bouillon and basil leaves, process for a further 2 minutes or until finely chopped. Add olive oil and process for 1 more minute. Refrigerate in a sealed jar.

Suitable to be frozen.

Nutritional Information	
PER SERVE (1 TEASPOON)	
CALORIES	9
TOTAL FAT	0.8g
SATURATED FAT	0.1g
SODIUM	6mg
CARBS	0.2g
SUGAR	0.1g
FIBER	0.2g
PROTEIN	0.3g
GI RATING	Low

PESTO PASTA SAUCE

Makes 4 servings

3.5fl oz (just over ⅓ cup) pesto (recipe above)

1 x 12½oz can low-fat 2% evaporated milk

To make this sauce you will need to prepare the recipe for LITE PESTO. Then measure a little more than a ⅓ of a cup of the pesto paste and place into a large saucepan. Add evaporated milk and combine well. Once sauce has boiled pour over cooked pasta and serve.

Suitable to be frozen for 2-3 weeks.

Nutritional Information	
PER SERVE	
CALORIES	108
TOTAL FAT	4.5g
SATURATED FAT	0.8g
SODIUM	148mg
CARBS	9.3g
SUGAR	9.1g
FIBER	0.6g
PROTEIN	7.4g
GI RATING	Low

Dietitian's tip

Pesto can be high in fat. At last a low-fat pesto sauce, what a treat.

CREAMY PUMPKIN & PINE NUT SAUCE

Makes 4 servings

2½ tablespoons pine nuts

1¼lb pumpkin or butternut squash peeled

cooking spray

½ cup onion finely diced

1 teaspoon crushed garlic (in jar)

1 teaspoon ground turmeric

1 tablespoon no-salt-added tomato paste

1 teaspoon ground cumin

1 teaspoon ground cilantro

2 teaspoons granulated vegetable stock powder (low sodium)

1 x 12½oz can low-fat 2% evaporated milk

pepper

Place pine nuts on a sheet of aluminum foil and brown under the griller, but be careful as they burn easily. Remove nuts and leave to one side. Cut pumpkin into large cubes then place in a microwave-safe dish with a little water and microwave for 6-7 minutes or until just cooked.

Coat a non-stick saucepan with cooking spray and sauté onion and garlic for 2 minutes. Add turmeric, tomato paste, cumin, cilantro and bouillon and cook 1 minute. Stir in evaporated milk and combine well. Add pepper to taste. Add in drained cooked pumpkin/squash and gently fold together. Bring to boil and serve over pasta. Sprinkle pine nuts over each serve.

Variations: Add ¾lb raw skinless chicken breast diced when sautéing onion and garlic until chicken is cooked, follow remainder of recipe as above or omit pine nuts to reduce the fat count by 3.5g per serve.

Suitable to be frozen for 2-3 weeks.

Nutritional Information

PER SERVE	PUMPKIN	CHICKEN
CALORIES	164	260
TOTAL FAT	5.8g	7.8g
SATURATED FAT	0.6g	1.1g
SODIUM	122mg	169mg
CARBS	19.6g	19.6g
SUGAR	15.2g	15.2g
FIBER	2.0g	2.0g
PROTEIN	9.8g	29.0g
GI RATING	Low	Low

Dietitian's tip

A delicious meat-free pasta sauce, everyone will love this one.

SMOKED SALMON CREAM SAUCE

Makes 4 servings

⅓ cup green onions sliced

⅓ cup white wine

1 teaspoon French mustard (in jar)

1 tablespoon lemon juice

½ teaspoon dried dill

1 x 12½oz can low-fat 2% evaporated milk

2 tablespoons no-salt-added tomato paste

5oz smoked salmon in strips

3 tablespoons cornstarch

1 cup no-fat milk

In a non-stick saucepan cook green onions, wine, mustard, lemon juice and dill, bring to boil then pour in evaporated milk. Add tomato paste and salmon and combine ingredients well. Mix cornstarch and no-fat milk, add to pan, when boiled pour over pasta.

Suitable to be frozen for 2-3 weeks.

Nutritional Information	
PER SERVE	
CALORIES	208
TOTAL FAT	5.9g
SATURATED FAT	1.3g
SODIUM	470mg
CARBS	18.7g
SUGAR	13.4g
FIBER	0.2g
PROTEIN	9.0g
GI RATING	Low

Dietitian's tip

Using low-fat evaporated milk is a great alternative to cream in sauces.

BEEF ITALIAN SAUCE

Makes 6 servings

1 cup red bell peppers large diced

1 cup small broccoli florets

1 cup zucchini sliced

1 cup fresh tomatoes diced

2 cups mushrooms sliced

Make a batch of Bolognaise Sauce on page 151. Leave in saucepan.

Microwave bell peppers, broccoli and zucchini in a little water on high for 5 minutes. Drain then add into the saucepan with bolognaise sauce and combine. Add tomatoes and mushrooms then cook a further 5 minutes. Fold cooked pasta into sauce until heated through then serve.

Suitable to be frozen.

Nutritional Information	
PER SERVE	
CALORIES	145
TOTAL FAT	3.4g
SATURATED FAT	1.3g
SODIUM	80mg
CARBS	8.6g
SUGAR	6.4g
FIBER	3.3g
PROTEIN	19.3g
GI RATING	Low

Dietitian's tip

Adding vegetables and pasta as a source of low Glycemic Index carbohydrates makes this a suitable meal for people with diabetes.

CHOCOLATE MOUSSE PIE

Makes 12 servings

Base

12 reduced-fat choc chip cookies (Nabisco®)

1 tablespoon light margarine melted (Promise®)

¾ teaspoon no-fat milk

cooking spray

Filling

3oz dark cooking chocolate

1 x 12½oz can low-fat 2% evaporated milk

½ teaspoon vanilla extract

2 tablespoons gelatin

½ cup boiling water

3 envelopes Swiss Miss Diet hot cocoa mix

Before getting started place canned milk into freezer for 1 hour before making filling.

To make base: In a food processor crumble cookies. Add melted margarine and milk, process until combined. Coat a 9" pie dish with cooking spray then spread cookie base over pie dish, pressing down firmly. Refrigerate.

To make filling: In a small ceramic bowl melt chocolate in microwave on high temperature for one minute. Leave to sit in microwave while you prepare other ingredients. Remember to make sure evaporated milk is very cold. In a large mixing bowl beat chilled milk and vanilla extract using an electric mixer until mixture has become really thick.

Using a whisk dissolve gelatin completely in boiling water then add melted chocolate and combine well. Add Swiss Miss envelopes to chocolate and combine well. Pour chocolate mixture into milk, beat continuously until well combined. Pour mixture over cookie base, refrigerate until set.

Variation: To make chocolate mousse omit base. Makes 8 servings.

Not suitable to be frozen.

Nutritional Information

PER SERVE	PIE	MOUSSE
CALORIES	124	73
TOTAL FAT	4.6g	2.5g
SATURATED FAT	2.0g	1.2g
SODIUM	139mg	81mg
CARBS	16.1g	8.4g
SUGAR	10.8g	7.2g
FIBER	0.7g	0.3g
PROTEIN	4.8g	4.2g
GI RATING	Low	Low

Dietitian's tip

A great low-fat dessert for all chocolate lovers.

BANANA CARAMEL
SELF SAUCING PUDDING

Makes 10 servings

Pudding

2 egg whites

¼ cup dark brown sugar

½ teaspoon baking soda

½ cup apple sauce (in jar)

¾ cup mashed banana (2 medium bananas)

1½ cups self-rising flour

Sauce

1 cup dark brown sugar

1½ cups water

Preheat oven to 350°F (180°C) fan forced.

To make pudding: In a medium size mixing bowl beat egg whites and sugar for 1 minute using an electric mixer. Stir baking soda into apple sauce (it will froth) then add to bowl. Add mashed bananas and combine. Gently fold flour into mixture in one go, DO NOT BEAT as this will make the pudding tough. Pour pudding mixture into a casserole dish (8 cup capacity).

To make caramel sauce: Sprinkle 1 cup of dark brown sugar over top of mixture and then gently pour water over the top. Bake 30-35 minutes or until firm to touch in centre.

Suitable to be frozen.

Nutritional Information

PER SERVE

CALORIES	160
TOTAL FAT	0.3g
SATURATED FAT	0g
SODIUM	216mg
CARBS	37.3g
SUGAR	22.1g
FIBER	1.1g
PROTEIN	3.0g
GI RATING	Medium

Dietitian's tip

Who doesn't love pudding? People with diabetes can enjoy this one but go for a smaller serve.

BAKED CHEESECAKE WITH BLUEBERRY SAUCE

Makes 12 servings

Base

15 oatmeal cookies sugar free (Mothers®)

1 tablespoon no-fat milk

cooking spray

Filling

1 x 16oz tub low-fat cottage cheese 2% milk fat

1 x 4oz ⅓ less fat Philadelphia® cream cheese

1 tablespoon grated lemon rind

3 tablespoons fresh lemon juice

1 teaspoon vanilla extract

¾ cup sugar

2 egg whites

1 whole egg

3 tablespoons all purpose flour

Syrup

1 x 15oz can blueberries in light syrup

1 tablespoon cornstarch

Preheat oven to 325°F (160°C) fan forced.

To make base: In a food processor crumble cookies, add milk and blend together. Coat a spring-based cake pan (8") with cooking spray and press base mix onto base of pan using the palm of your hand. Refrigerate while making the filling.

To make filling: Clean food processor bowl and add cottage cheese, blend until very smooth, add cream cheese and blend. Finely chop rind then add to processor with lemon juice and extract, blend ingredients. Slowly add in sugar until dissolved. Add egg whites and egg and combine with mixture, add flour. Once combined pour mixture over cookie base. Bake for 1 hour. Remove from the oven then release the spring of cake pan to loosen cheesecake away from the edge. This may help stop the filling from cracking as it cools.

To make syrup: Place both ingredients into a small saucepan and bring to boil, stirring continuously. Leave to cool. Pour equal amounts of sauce over each serving.

Variation: Omit blueberry sauce for a plain cheesecake or replace canned blueberries with any canned fruit of your choice.

Not suitable to be frozen.

Nutritional Information

PER SERVE	WITH SAUCE	PLAIN
CALORIES	185	153
TOTAL FAT	4.4g	4.4g
SATURATED FAT	2.0g	2.0g
SODIUM	226mg	225mg
CARBS	29.1g	21.5g
SUGAR	18.0g	13.1g
FIBER	1.0g	0.4g
PROTEIN	7.8g	7.1g
GI RATING	Medium	Medium

Dietitian's tip

This one's a winner. Everyone will love this low-fat cheesecake!

STRABERRIES ROMANNETTE

Makes 4 servings

2 x 4oz tubs vanilla pudding
1% milk (Kozy Shack®)

2 x 6oz tubs no-fat vanilla yogurt

1 tablespoon orange juice

2 tablespoons Cointreau liqueur

8oz fresh strawberries chopped

For a stronger flavour, marinate fruit with liqueur for 1-2 hours but it is not necessary. Place vanilla pudding and yogurt into a medium size mixing bowl and combine. Pour juice and Cointreau into mix and fold together. Place strawberries into mix and combine well. Refrigerate until required.

Variations: Replace strawberries with any fresh or frozen berries or replace liqueur with liqueur of your choice. Or replace vanilla flavored yogurt with strawberry flavored yogurt.

Suitable to be frozen for 2-3 weeks.

Dietitian's tip

This fruit dessert is low in fat and has a low Glycemic Index making it ideal for people with diabetes.

BLUEBERRY PANCAKES
Makes 6 pancakes

Pancake mix

1 x 15oz can blueberries in light syrup

2 egg whites

¼ cup sugar

¼ teaspoon vanilla extract

½ cup no-fat milk

1 cup self-rising flour

½ teaspoon baking soda

cooking spray

Syrup

saved juice from canned blueberries

1 tablespoon cornstarch

To make pancake mix: Drain blueberries, save juice from can to make sauce. In a medium size mixing bowl beat egg whites and sugar for a minute using an electric mixer. Add vanilla extract and milk and mix. Sift flour and baking soda into mixture in one go, DO NOT BEAT but gently fold flour through until just combined (over beating bruises the flour and will make the pancakes tough). Fold blueberries through the batter gently.

Coat a non-stick frypan with cooking spray and pour a little less than half a cup of mixture into pan, spread batter to make a round shape. Cook 1-2 minutes or until browned, turn and cook another minute or so until cooked. Repeat until all mixture has been used.

To make syrup: In a small saucepan combine the saved syrup and cornstarch, stir continuously on medium heat. Once boiled pour syrup over each pancake.

Variations: Omit the blueberry syrup and reduce carbohydrate count to 33.4g, calories drop to 154.
For apple pancakes replace can of blueberries with 2 cups fresh apple peeled and finely diced.
Instead of syrup make cinnamon sugar by mixing 4 teaspoons sugar and 1 teaspoon cinnamon together, sprinkle over pancakes.

Suitable to be frozen.

Nutritional Information

PER PANCAKE	BERRY	APPLE
CALORIES	183	149
TOTAL FAT	0.3g	0.4g
SATURATED FAT	0.1g	0.1g
SODIUM	283mg	281mg
CARBS	40.1g	32.6g
SUGAR	18.2g	15.9g
FIBER	2.0g	1.7g
PROTEIN	9.5g	4.3g
GI RATING	Medium	Medium

Dietitian's tip

A great Sunday breakfast that is also a source of fiber.

CHOCOLATE FUDGE SAUCE

Makes 12 servings

4oz dairy milk cooking chocolate

**1 x 12½oz can low-fat
2% evaporated milk**

2 tablespoons cocoa powder

1 tablespoon cornstarch

**3 envelopes Swiss Miss®
Diet Hot Cocoa Mix**

Break or cut chocolate into small pieces. In a medium size saucepan whisk together milk, cocoa, cornstarch and Swiss Miss envelopes until blended. Cook on med-high stirring continuously until mixture just boils. Remove from heat then add in chocolate, whisk together well until the chocolate has melted. Allow 2 tablespoons per serve.

Variation: For a darker chocolate sauce replace milk chocolate with dark cooking chocolate.

Not suitable to be frozen.

Nutritional Information	
PER SERVE	
CALORIES	85
TOTAL FAT	3.2g
SATURATED FAT	1.7g
SODIUM	83mg
CARBS	10.6g
SUGAR	8.7g
FIBER	0.4g
PROTEIN	3.4g
GI RATING	Low

Dietitian's tip

Yum, this sauce is perfect over low-fat ice-cream or poured over fruit salad. Enjoy this in moderation.

CREAMY COCONUT RICE
Makes 6 servings

¾ cup uncooked short grain rice

4 cups no-fat milk

¼ cup sugar

¼ teaspoon imitation
coconut extract

1 tablespoon shredded coconut

Rinse starch off rice. Pour milk and sugar into a medium size saucepan and bring to boil, stir occasionally. Keep on a medium heat so the milk doesn't burn on bottom of pan.

Add rice and once boiling, reduce to slow boil until rice is cooked (about 20-25 minutes). Stir rice frequently to avoid burning or sticking to pot. Add coconut extract and coconut. Serve hot or cold. If mixture gets too thick add a little more no-fat milk. Serve on its own or with canned fruit in natural juice or stewed fruit.

Variation: For plain creamy rice omit coconut extract and coconut.

Not suitable to be frozen.

Nutritional Information

PER SERVE	COCONUT	PLAIN
CALORIES	173	169
TOTAL FAT	0.8g	0.3g
SATURATED FAT	0.7g	0.2g
SODIUM	70mg	70mg
CARBS	35.2g	35.2g
SUGAR	15.7g	15.7g
FIBER	0.3g	0.2g
PROTEIN	7.2g	7.1g
GI RATING	Medium	Medium

Dietitian's tip

Again coconut extract is used to reduce the fat content and make it suitable for people with diabetes.

FRUIT 'N' NUT COBBLER

Makes 8 servings

Filling

2lb green apples

¼ cup water

2 teaspoons sugar

1 x 14½oz can peaches in natural juice drained

Topping

1½ cups Special K® cereal

½ cup self-rising flour

¼ cup rolled oats

⅓ cup brown sugar

¼ teaspoon cinnamon

¼ cup pecan nuts

2 tablespoons light margarine melted (Promise®)

1 teaspoon no-fat milk

Preheat oven to 350°F (180°C) fan forced.

To make filling: Peel and cut apples into quarters. Remove core then cut each quarter into 3 slices (4 for very large apples). Place in a large microwave dish with ¼ cup water and sugar. Microwave on high for 6 minutes for 1200 watt microwave or 8 minutes for lower watt microwaves or until apple is just cooked but still firm. Drain apples and peaches then spread over the base of a casserole or small lasagne dish. Combine fruits together.

To make topping: In a medium size mixing bowl crush Special K using either potato masher or your fist. Add flour, oats, sugar and cinnamon. Chop pecan nuts into small pieces then add to bowl and combine well. Add melted margarine to milk then pour into bowl and combine with dry ingredients. You may find using your hand to combine mixture works best. Sprinkle mixture over top of fruit. Bake 30 minutes or until browned.

Variations: Replace suggested fruit with any fruit of your choice or replace Special K with bran flakes or corn flakes.

Not suitable to be frozen.

Nutritional Information

PER SERVE	
CALORIES	167
TOTAL FAT	4.2g
SATURATED FAT	0.5g
SODIUM	132mg
CARBS	29.5g
SUGAR	17.2g
FIBER	2.3g
PROTEIN	3.3g
GI RATING	Medium

Dietitian's tip

Peaches and apples have a low Glycemic Index and are an ideal dessert for people with diabetes.

FRUIT DE-LIGHT

Makes 4 servings

1 x 12g envelope orange (or similar colored) sugar free jelly crystals

1 cup boiling water

1 x 14½oz can apricot halves in natural juice drained

2 x 6oz tubs no-fat apricot (or similar colored) yogurt

Dissolve jelly crystals in boiling water. Place drained apricots into a food processor/blender with jelly and blend together. Pour in yogurt and blend until combined well. Pour into dessert dishes then place in refrigerator to set.

Variation: Replace canned apricots with any canned fruit you like but match the color of fruit with jelly and yogurt (keep same quantities as with the apricot recipe).

Suitable to be frozen for 2-3 weeks.

Nutritional Information

PER SERVE	
CALORIES	76
TOTAL FAT	0.1g
SATURATED FAT	0.1g
SODIUM	51mg
CARBS	12.8g
SUGAR	4.3g
FIBER	1.5g
PROTEIN	5.3g
GI RATING	Low

Dietitian's tip

A low calorie dessert that will satisfy people with diabetes who aim to lose weight.

MISSISSIPPI MUD CAKE

Makes 14 servings

Cake

5oz dark cooking chocolate

4oz light margarine (Promise®)

1 cup sugar

2 teaspoons instant coffee

1 cup water

¼ cup bourbon or brandy

½ teaspoon baking soda

½ cup apple sauce (in jar)

2 egg whites

1½ cups all purpose flour

⅓ cup cocoa powder

cooking spray

Frosting

2 tablespoons cocoa powder

¾ cup confectioner's sugar

2 teaspoons light margarine (Promise®)

about 1 tablespoon no-fat milk

Preheat oven to 325°F (160°C) fan forced.

To make cake: Place chocolate, margarine, sugar, coffee, water and bourbon into a large ceramic dish and microwave on medium-low for 2 minutes. Stir ingredients then return to microwave for a further 2 minutes on medium-low. Stir until all ingredients are dissolved. Stir baking soda into apple sauce (it will froth) then add to chocolate mix.

In a cup beat egg whites using a fork then add to chocolate mix. Sift all the flour and cocoa into bowl then gently fold ingredients until combined. Pour mixture into an 8" round cake pan coated with cooking spray and bake for 55-60 minutes or until cake springs back when lightly pressed in center. When cool spread frosting over cake.

To make frosting: Sift cocoa and confectioner's sugar, add margarine and enough milk until a smooth frosting is made. Spread over cake. Refrigerate.

NOTE: Mississippi Mud Cakes have a tendency to crack a little on the top. The icing will camouflage this. A traditional mud cake has around 50g of fat a serve.

Suitable to be frozen.

Nutritional Information

PER SERVE

CALORIES	233
TOTAL FAT	6.6g
SATURATED FAT	2.6g
SODIUM	77mg
CARBS	38.8g
SUGAR	25.9g
FIBER	1.0g
PROTEIN	3.3g
GI RATING	Medium

Dietitian's tip

Everyone's favourite! People with diabetes enjoy this one only on special occasions.

PUMPKIN PIE

Makes 12 servings

Pastry

¼ cup self-rising flour

¾ cup all purpose flour

2 tablespoons sugar

2 tablespoons light margarine melted (Promise®)

1 tablespoon no-fat milk

1 egg white

cooking spray

Filling

3 cups (1lb) raw pumpkin or butternut squash small dice

2 whole eggs

2 egg whites

½ cup sugar

1 teaspoon cinnamon

1 teaspoon ground nutmeg

1½ cups no-fat milk

Preheat oven to 350°F (180°C) fan forced.

To make pastry: In a medium size mixing bowl combine flours and sugar together. Add melted margarine to milk, beat in egg white with a fork, pour into flour. Fold together; if needed use your hands to help blend ingredients. Place onto a well-floured surface and roll out to fit a 9" pie dish that has been coated with cooking spray. Roll up pastry using a rolling pin, lift into pie dish. Trim around edges.

To make filling: Microwave pumpkin with a little water on high for 10 minutes or until pumpkin is cooked. Drain and mash. Measure 1½ cups of cooked mashed pumpkin to use for recipe. In a large mixing bowl beat eggs and egg whites together with sugar for 1 minute using an electric mixer. Add pumpkin, cinnamon, nutmeg and milk mixing until well combined. Pour over pastry and bake for 1 hour 15 minutes. Leave to cool.

Not suitable to be frozen.

Nutritional Information

PER SERVE

CALORIES	112
TOTAL FAT	2.0g
SATURATED FAT	0.5g
SODIUM	74mg
CARBS	19.3g
SUGAR	10.4g
FIBER	0.6g
PROTEIN	4.6g
GI RATING	Medium

Dietitian's tip
Pumpkin is a good source of many vitamins and minerals. Dietary recommendations suggest 5 serves of vegetables a day to achieve good health.

LEMON MERINGUE PIE

Makes 10 servings

Pastry

1 cup self-rising flour

1 tablespoon sugar

1 tablespoon light margarine (Promise®)

2 tablespoons no-fat milk

1 egg white

flour to roll pastry

cooking spray

Filling

½ cup fresh lemon juice

½ cup sugar

½ cup water

5 tablespoons cornstarch

3-5 drops yellow food coloring

½ cup low-fat 2% evaporated milk

Meringue

3 egg whites

¾ cup sugar

Preheat oven to 350°F (180°C) fan forced.

To make pastry: In a medium size mixing bowl combine flour and sugar. Melt margarine and add to milk, using a fork beat egg white into milk mixture until combined. Pour into flour and fold together.

Place pastry on a well-floured surface and roll out to fit shape of round 9" pie dish that has been coated with cooking spray. Roll up pastry using a rolling pin, lift into pie dish. Trim around edges and bake 10-15 minutes or until lightly browned. Allow to cool.

To make filling: In a medium size saucepan heat all ingredients except evaporated milk. Using a whisk, blend ingredients together until mixture comes to the boil, whisk in evaporated milk. Leave to cool.

To make meringue: In a medium size mixing bowl beat egg whites using an electric mixer until stiff peaks form. Gradually add in sugar beating well each time until all sugar has been used.

To assemble pie: Spread lemon filling evenly over prepared pastry base. Spoon meringue mixture on top of filling, spreading to the edge of pie, make peaks with flat of spoon. Bake 10-15 minutes or until meringue has browned.

Not suitable to be frozen.

Nutritional Information

PER SERVE

CALORIES	174
TOTAL FAT	0.9g
SATURATED FAT	0.1g
SODIUM	145mg
CARBS	37.9g
SUGAR	24.6g
FIBER	0.5g
PROTEIN	3.7g
GI RATING	Medium

Dietitian's tip
This pie has much less fat than traditional recipes. This is great but the nutrient level is low and the carbohydrate and sugar intake are high so I advise people with diabetes to avoid this pie or have it very occasionally.

CRÈME CARAMELS

Makes 8 servings

Toffee topping

¾ cup sugar

¾ cup water

Custard

3 whole eggs

3 egg whites

3 cups no-fat milk

½ teaspoon vanilla extract

½ cup sugar

Preheat oven to 325°F (160°C) fan forced.

You will require 8 ovenproof ramekin pots (¾ cup capacity) to make the crème caramels in.

To make toffee: In a non-stick saucepan bring sugar and water to the boil, reduce heat slightly and continue on a slow boil for about 10-20 minutes (don't stir). Keep an eye on the toffee as it can burn quickly. Once the toffee is a golden brown colour remove from heat and pour equal amounts into each of the ramekins. Leave to one side.

To make the custard: Place whole eggs and egg whites into a large mixing bowl and beat until blended, add in all other ingredients and beat until well combined. Pour equal amounts of custard into the 8 ramekins. Place in a large baking pan that has been half filled with water. Depending on size of ramekins bake for 50-60 minutes or until custard is firm to touch. Leave to cool. To remove from ramekins use a sharp knife around edge of custard, turn ramekin over onto dessert plate and holding the plate and the ramekin together shake down to release crème caramel.

Not suitable to be frozen.

Nutritional Information

PER SERVE

CALORIES	165
TOTAL FAT	1.9g
SATURATED FAT	0.7g
SODIUM	83mg
CARBS	32.0g
SUGAR	32.1g
FIBER	0g
PROTEIN	6.7g
GI RATING	Medium

Dietitian's tip

This is a great alternative to traditional crème caramel. People with diabetes save this one for special occasions.

ANNIE'S APPLE PIE
Makes 12 servings

Filling

3lb green apples

⅓ cup water

2 tablespoons sugar

4 whole cloves (optional)

Pastry

2½ cups self-rising flour

1 tablespoon sugar

2oz light margarine (Promise®)

½ cup no-fat milk

1 egg white

flour to roll pastry

cooking spray

a little no-fat milk

1 teaspoon sugar

Preheat oven to 350°F (180°C) fan forced.

To make filling: Peel and cut apples into quarters. Remove core then cut each quarter into 3 slices. Place into a large saucepan or boiler with water, sugar and cloves. Cook for around 6-8 minutes or until apple is just cooked but still firm. Drain then leave to cool.

To make pastry: In a large mixing bowl combine flour and sugar together. Melt margarine, stir into milk, then using a fork beat egg white into milk mixture until combined. Pour milk mixture into flour and gently fold together. Divide in 2, placing one half on a well-floured bench. Roll out pastry to fit a round 9" pie dish. Place rolled pastry over base of pie dish that has been coated with cooking spray.

Remove cloves from apple mix then spread apples evenly over top of pastry. Roll out remaining pastry to fit over top of apple to reach edge of pie plate. Using a sharp knife trim hanging edges. Pinch the edges together with your finger and thumb or use a fork and press edges together, brush top of pastry with a little milk, sprinkle a teaspoon of sugar over top. Cut a small slit in centre of pastry. Bake 40-45 minutes or until golden brown.

Suitable to be frozen.

Nutritional Information

PER SERVE	
CALORIES	158
TOTAL FAT	2.2g
SATURATED FAT	0.4g
SODIUM	252mg
CARBS	30.8g
SUGAR	9.0g
FIBER	2.1g
PROTEIN	3.8g
GI RATING	Medium

Dietitian's tip
Annette has made a low-fat pastry, plus the apple filling adds vitamins, minerals and fiber making this dessert a nutritious occasional dessert for people with diabetes.

Baking

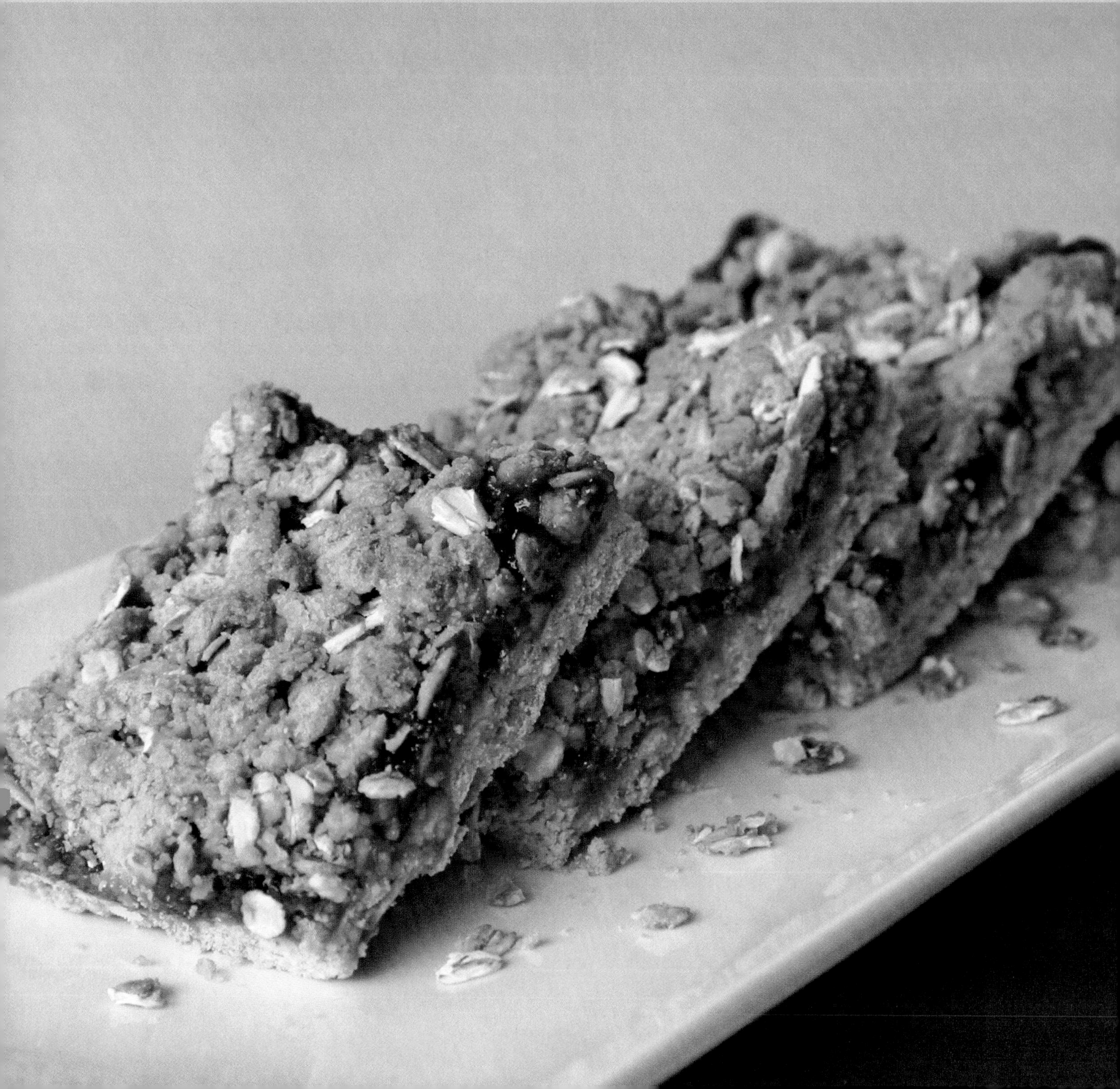

JAM CRUMBLE SLICE

Makes 15 serves

2 cups self-rising flour

⅓ cup brown sugar

1 cup raw rolled oats

6 tablespoons light margarine (Promise®)

¼ cup no fat milk

cooking spray

¾ cup raspberry jam

Preheat oven to 350°F (180°C) fan forced.

In a large mixing bowl combine all dry ingredients. Melt margarine, mix together with milk and add to dry mix. Mix all ingredients together well. In a 9" x 9" baking pan that has been coated with cooking spray place a little more than half the mixture over the base, pressing down with the palm of your hand.

Warm jam slightly in microwave then spread evenly over base. Sprinkle remaining dough over jam then press down with your hand or the back of a large spoon until mixture is flattened. Bake 30-35 minutes or until golden brown on top. When cool cut into slices.

Variation: Swap raspberry jam with any jam of your choice.

Suitable to be frozen.

Nutritional Information

PER SERVE

CALORIES	148
TOTAL FAT	2.6g
SATURATED FAT	0.5g
SODIUM	173mg
CARBS	29.1g
SUGAR	14.5g
FIBER	1.1g
PROTEIN	2.4g
GI RATING	Medium

Dietitian's tip

Rolled oats have a low Glycemic Index, making this slice a suitable choice for people with diabetes.

CARAMEL TARTS

Makes 24 tarts

Pastry

¾ cup all purpose flour

¼ cup self-rising flour

2 tablespoons sugar

2 tablespoons light margarine (Promise®)

1 tablespoon no fat milk

1 egg white

extra all purpose flour to roll pastry

cooking spray

Caramel filling

1 cup low-fat 2% evaporated milk

1 x 14oz can fat-free condensed milk

2 tablespoons light margarine (Promise®)

¼ cup brown sugar

1 tablespoon cornstarch

¼ cup water

Preheat oven to 350°F (180°C) fan forced.

To make pastry: Place flours and sugar in a medium size mixing bowl. Melt margarine and add to milk. Using a fork beat egg white into milk until combined, pour into flour and fold together. Place pastry on to a well-floured surface and roll thinly.

Using a 3" scone cutter, cut out 24 pastry bases. Place 12 bases into a cup cake or a muffin pan that has been coated with cooking spray. Bake 10 minutes or until lightly browned, remove and cool on a wire rack. Wash tray and repeat procedure with remaining 12 pastry bases.

To make filling: In a small mixing bowl whisk together evaporated milk and condensed milk, leave to one side. In a non-stick saucepan melt margarine, add in brown sugar and combine, once sugar has dissolved remove from heat and whisk in the milk mixture.

Place back on stove and bring to boil on a medium-high temperature, stir continuously so as not to burn bottom of pan. Once boiled reduce to a slow boil until mixture is a rich caramel colour, about 15-20 minutes (do longer if not thickened), stirring frequently. Dissolve cornstarch in ¼ cup of water and stir into pan, once boiled remove from heat and allow to cool. Spoon equal amounts of filling into pastry cases.

Pastry cases are suitable to be frozen.

Nutritional Information

PER TART	
CALORIES	60
TOTAL FAT	1.1g
SATURATED FAT	0.3g
SODIUM	59mg
CARBS	18.2g
SUGAR	13.7g
FIBER	0.2g
PROTEIN	2.9g
GI RATING	Medium

Dietitian's tip

Sheer indulgence! Enjoy a delicious tart but keep in mind that it offers little nutritional value.

CARROT CAKE

Makes 12 servings

Cake

2 egg whites

⅓ cup sugar

½ cup apple sauce (in jar)

⅓ cup raisins

1 cup carrot grated

¼ cup walnuts chopped

1 teaspoon ground ginger

2 teaspoons orange rind grated

¾ teaspoon baking soda

¼ cup warm water

1½ cups self-rising flour

cooking spray

Frosting

¾ cup confectioner's sugar

1 teaspoon light margarine (Promise®)

1-2 teaspoons fresh orange juice

Preheat oven to 350°F (180°C) fan forced.

To make cake: Beat egg whites and sugar together in medium size mixing bowl for 1 minute using an electric mixer. Stir in apple sauce, raisins, carrots, walnuts, ginger and rind to egg mix. Dissolve baking soda in warm water, add to mix. Gently fold flour into mixture in one go. DO NOT BEAT as this will make the cake tough.

Once flour is combined (mixture can look a little lumpy) pour into an 8" round cake or loaf pan that has been coated with cooking spray. Bake 35-40 minutes or until cake springs back when lightly pressed in center. Let cake stand for 5 minutes before turning onto cake rack.

To make frosting: Mix confectioner's sugar and margarine in a small mixing bowl, slowly add enough juice to make a spreadable consistency. Spread over top of cake. Sprinkle extra grated orange rind or a little cinnamon over frosting for decoration (optional).

Suitable to be frozen preferably without the frosting.

Nutritional Information

PER SERVE	PLAIN	WITH FROSTING
CALORIES	123	158
TOTAL FAT	1.7g	1.9g
SATURATED FAT	0.1g	0.2g
SODIUM	184mg	188mg
CARBS	24.2g	32.9g
SUGAR	11.6g	20.1g
FIBER	1.4g	1.4g
PROTEIN	2.9g	2.9g
GI RATING	Medium	Medium

Dietitian's tip

Occasionally have this nutrient dense cake but avoid the icing if you are overweight, have diabetes or heart disease.

CHOC CHIP COOKIES

Makes 24 Cookies

1 egg white

½ cup sugar

4 tablespoons light margarine (Promise®)

¼ cup no-fat milk

½ teaspoon vanilla extract

½ cup choc chips roughly chopped

1½ cups self-rising flour

cooking spray

Preheat oven to 350°F (180°C) fan forced.

In a medium size mixing bowl beat egg white and sugar for 1 minute using an electric mixer. Melt margarine then add to milk, pour into bowl with vanilla extract and choc chips. Stir sifted flour into mix, combine well.

Drop a dessertspoon of mixture onto a flat baking pan that has been coated with cooking spray allowing for room to spread. Flatten each spoonful with the back of a fork that has been dipped in boiling water. Bake 20-25 minutes. Leave to cool on tray.

Variation: For double choc chip cookies add ¼ cup sifted cocoa powder in with the flour.

Not suitable to be frozen.

Nutritional Information

PER COOKIE	CHOC	DOUBLE CHOC
CALORIES	72	75
TOTAL FAT	2.1g	2.2g
SATURATED FAT	0.8g	0.9g
SODIUM	81mg	84mg
CARBS	12.3g	12.5g
SUGAR	5.7g	5.7g
FIBER	0.4g	0.4g
PROTEIN	1.3g	1.5g
GI RATING	Medium	Medium

Dietitian's tip

Not much in the way of nutritional value but is low in fat and calories. These cookies can be included in the eating plan of a person with diabetes occasionally.

CHOCOLATE SLICE

Makes 15 slices

Base

1 cup self-rising flour

¼ cup cocoa powder

2 Weetabix® crushed

½ cup sugar

2 tablespoons shredded coconut

4 tablespoons light margarine melted (Promise®)

2 tablespoons no-fat milk

1 egg white

cooking spray

Frosting

¾ cup confectioner's sugar

1 tablespoon cocoa powder

1 teaspoon light margarine (Promise®)

2-3 teaspoons no-fat milk

1½ teaspoons shredded coconut (optional)

Preheat oven 350°F (180°C) fan forced.

To make base: Sift flour and cocoa into a large mixing bowl with crushed Weetabix, sugar and coconut. Add melted margarine to milk. Using a fork beat egg white into milk until combined, pour into flour and fold together. Spread mixture over the base of a 9" x 9" baking pan that has been coated with cooking spray. Use the palm of your hand to flatten and spread mixture. You may need to dip your hand into flour to avoid mixture sticking. Bake for 35 minutes.

To make frosting: Sift confectioner's sugar and cocoa into a small mixing bowl. Add margarine and milk, blend well. Spread over slice while base is still warm. Sprinkle coconut over top, leave to cool. Cut into 15 slices.

Not suitable to be frozen.

Nutritional Information

PER SLICE

CALORIES	113
TOTAL FAT	2.5g
SATURATED FAT	0.9g
SODIUM	107mg
CARBS	21.2g
SUGAR	12.9g
FIBER	0.8g
PROTEIN	1.9g
GI RATING	Medium

Dietitian's tip
Wow, I love the taste of chocolate. This is low in fat but also low on the nutrient front. Don't go back for seconds - definitely a special occasion food.

CRUNCHY COOKIES

Makes 15 cookies

6 tablespoons light margarine (Promise®)

⅓ cup sugar

1 egg white

2 tablespoons shredded coconut

½ cup raisins

1 cup self-rising flour

2 tablespoons no-fat milk

2 cups corn flakes

cooking spray

Preheat oven to 350°F (180°C) fan forced.

In a large mixing bowl beat margarine and sugar using an electric mixer until sugar has dissolved. Add egg white and beat, fold in coconut, raisins, flour and milk, mix together. Fold in corn flakes until ingredients are combined.

Drop a dessertspoon of mixture onto a flat baking pan that has been coated with cooking spray. Repeat process until 15 cookies are formed. Flatten each cookie. Bake 20 minutes or until golden brown. Cool on wire rack.

Variations: For a plain biscuit omit raisins and add ½ teaspoon vanilla extract, or replace raisins with currants or with ½ cup chocolate chips.

Not suitable to be frozen.

Nutritional Information

PER COOKIE	CRUNCHY	PLAIN	CHOC
CALORIES	103	86	115
TOTAL FAT	2.7g	2.7g	4.3g
SATURATED FAT	0.8g	0.8g	2.4g
SODIUM	155mg	153mg	155mg
CARBS	18.2g	13.9g	17.3g
SUGAR	8.5g	4.4g	7.4g
FIBER	0.8g	0.6g	0.6g
PROTEIN	1.7g	1.5g	1.7g
GI RATING	Medium	Medium	Medium

Dietitian's tip

A great snack food for people who have diabetes – resist the second one!

HUMMINGBIRD CAKE

Makes 12 servings

Cake

¾ cup canned crushed pineapple (in natural juice)

2 egg whites

¼ cup sugar

¾ teaspoon baking soda

½ cup apple sauce (in jar)

1 cup mashed ripe banana

¼ cup walnuts chopped

1 teaspoon ground mixed spice

2 cups self-rising flour

cooking spray

Frosting

¾ cup confectioner's sugar

about 2 teaspoons pineapple juice (saved from canned pineapple)

1 teaspoon light margarine (Promise®)

Preheat oven to 350°F (180°C) fan forced.

To make cake: Drain pineapple keeping juice for frosting. In a large mixing bowl beat egg whites and sugar for 1 minute using an electric mixer. Stir baking soda into apple sauce (it will froth) and add to bowl. Mix in mashed banana, walnuts, drained pineapple and mixed spice, blend ingredients together well. Gently fold sifted flour into mixture in one go, treat this mixture as if a sponge, DO NOT BEAT as this will make the cake tough.

Pour mixture into an 8" round cake pan that has been coated with cooking spray. Bake 35-40 minutes or until firm to touch in center. Allow cake to sit for 5 minutes in pan before turning onto a wire rack to cool.

To make frosting: Once cake has cooled place all frosting ingredients into a small mixing bowl, combine until smooth. Spread over top of cake.

NOTE: In humid weather it is best to keep this cake refrigerated.

Suitable to be frozen preferably without frosting.

Nutritional Information

PER SERVE

CALORIES	182
TOTAL FAT	1.9g
SATURATED FAT	0.2g
SODIUM	177mg
CARBS	37.9g
SUGAR	20.3g
FIBER	1.7g
PROTEIN	3.6g
GI RATING	Low

Dietitian's tip

Annette, you have done it again! This is a fantastic low-fat alternative to traditional Hummingbird cake. People with diabetes can enjoy a small serve.

PINEAPPLE FRUIT CAKE

Makes 16 servings

1¼ cups raisins

1¼ cups currants

½ cup candied cherries cut in half

1 teaspoon ground mixed spice

⅓ cup water

1 x 15oz can crushed pineapple (in natural juice)

¾ teaspoon baking soda

3 egg whites

2 cups self-rising flour

cooking spray

In a medium size saucepan place dried fruit, cherries, spice, water and whole can of pineapple, bring to boil, simmer for 3 minutes. Stir in baking soda and pour into medium size mixing bowl to cool.

Preheat oven to 350°F (180°C) fan forced.

Once fruit mixture has cooled beat egg whites into fruit. Sift flour into bowl in one go and fold until combined. Pour mixture into an 8" round cake pan or large loaf pan that has been coated with cooking spray and bake approximately 1 hour or until firm in center. Allow cake to sit 5 minutes in pan before turning onto a wire rack to cool.

Suitable to be frozen.

Nutritional Information

PER SERVE

CALORIES	163
TOTAL FAT	0.3g
SATURATED FAT	0.1g
SODIUM	178mg
CARBS	37.2g
SUGAR	24.4g
FIBER	2.4g
PROTEIN	3.3g
GI RATING	Low

Dietitian's tip
This recipe contains carbohydrates and calories but also has a high nutritional value. Many people with diabetes may find that this is not suitable for them.

PEAR & CRANBERRY LOAF
Makes 12 servings

2 small fresh pears

2 egg whites

⅓ cup sugar

½ cup light cranberry juice

½ teaspoon baking soda

½ teaspoon cinnamon

½ cup dried cranberries

2 tablespoons light margarine melted (Promise®)

1¾ cups self-rising flour

cooking spray

Preheat oven to 350°F (180°C) fan forced.

Peel and core pears, then cut into small dice. In a medium size mixing bowl beat egg whites and sugar for 1 minute using an electric mixer. Add diced pears, cranberry juice, baking soda, cinnamon, cranberries and melted margarine. Combine well.

Sift flour into bowl in one go and gently fold mixture until flour is just combined, DO NOT BEAT as this will make the loaf tough. Pour mixture into a large loaf pan that has been coated with cooking spray. Bake for 30-35 minutes or until cooked in center. Turn onto a wire rack to cool.

Variation: Replace pear with fresh diced apple.

Suitable to be frozen.

Nutritional Information
PER SERVE

CALORIES	123
TOTAL FAT	1.1g
SATURATED FAT	0.2g
SODIUM	213mg
CARBS	25.7g
SUGAR	10.6g
FIBER	1.3g
PROTEIN	2.6g
GI RATING	Medium

Dietitian's tip

A loaf which is full of fruit and so low in fat, great to serve to your guests who like to eat healthy tasty food.

CHOCOLATE PEPPERMINT CRACKLES

Makes 18 crackles

3 cups Rice Krispies®

3 x 3 Musketeers® mint bars 45% less fat (35.2g per bar)

4 tablespoons light margarine (Promise®)

2 tablespoons dark corn syrup

18 paper cup cake cases

Place Rice Krispies into a large mixing bowl. Roughly chop mint bars then place in a small microwave-safe bowl with margarine and corn syrup. Melt on high for 2 minutes, give mixture a good stir.

Pour into Rice Krispies and fold together until ingredients are well coated. Place paper cases into muffin or cup cake pans then spoon an equal amount of mixture into each paper case. Place into refrigerator to set. To keep crackles firm keep refrigerated.

Not suitable to be frozen.

Nutritional Information

PER CRACKLE

CALORIES	60
TOTAL FAT	2.0g
SATURATED FAT	0.8g
SODIUM	87mg
CARBS	10.1g
SUGAR	4.8g
FIBER	0.2g
PROTEIN	0.4g
GI RATING	Medium

Dietitian's tip

A real chocolate treat but has very little nutritional value.

PIKELETS
Makes 24 pikelets

2 egg whites

2 tablespoons sugar

½ teaspoon white vinegar

1 cup no-fat milk

1 tablespoon light
margarine (Promise®)

1½ cups self-rising flour

cooking spray

In a medium size mixing bowl beat egg whites and sugar for 30 seconds using an electric mixer. Add vinegar to milk (don't worry if the milk curdles). Melt margarine then pour into milk. Add to bowl and combine. Sift flour into mixture in one go and fold gently, DO NOT BEAT as this will make the pikelets tough.

Coat frypan generously with cooking spray then drop spoonfuls of mixture onto hot frypan. When mixture starts bubbling turn pikelets over and cook other side for a few minutes. Repeat this step spraying with cooking spray each time until all mixture has been used. Makes approximately 24 pikelets.

Variation: For fruit pikelets add ½ cup raisins (or any other dried fruit of your choice) to mix before flour is added to bowl.

Suitable to be frozen.

Nutritional Information

PER PIKELET	PLAIN	RAISIN
CALORIES	40	50
TOTAL FAT	0.3g	0.3g
SATURATED FAT	0.1g	0.1g
SODIUM	73mg	75mg
CARBS	7.5g	10.2g
SUGAR	1.4g	4.0g
FIBER	0.3g	0.5g
PROTEIN	1.5g	1.6g
GI RATING	Too low in carbs to score a rating	

Dietitian's tip

Add mixed berries and low fat yogurt for a healthy dessert for people with diabetes.

SYMPLE JUMBLE COOKIES
Makes 24 cookies

1 egg white

⅓ cup sugar

¼ cup no-fat milk

2 tablespoons honey

½ teaspoon vanilla extract

4 tablespoons light margarine melted (Promise®)

1 teaspoon ground allspice

1 teaspoon ground mixed spice

1 teaspoon ground ginger

2 teaspoons ground cinnamon

1½ cups self-rising flour

cooking spray

Frosting

1 small freezer bag

½ cup confectioner's sugar sifted

a little no-fat milk

red food coloring (optional)

Preheat oven to 350°F (180°C) fan forced.

In a medium size mixing bowl beat egg white and sugar for 1 minute using an electric mixer. Add milk, honey and vanilla extract to melted margarine and place in bowl, combine together. Add spices and mix together then fold flour into mix.

Spoon 24 tablespoons of cookie dough onto flat baking pan that has been coated with cooking spray. Dip a fork into boiling water then lightly press the dough flat (this stops the dough from sticking to the fork). Bake for 20-25 minutes or until golden brown. Leave to cool.

To make frosting: Carefully snip a tiny part off a bottom corner of the plastic bag. In a small mixing bowl combine enough milk with confectioner's sugar until a slightly runny consistency. Add a few drops of coloring to mixture to give frosting a pink color (optional). Spoon into bag. Squeeze a little frosting in a squiggle fashion over each cookie. Leave to set.

Not suitable to be frozen.

Nutritional Information
PER COOKIE

CALORIES	66
TOTAL FAT	1.1g
SATURATED FAT	0.2g
SODIUM	80mg
CARBS	13.2g
SUGAR	6.8g
FIBER	0.3g
PROTEIN	1.2g
GI RATING	Medium

Dietitian's tip

This delightful spicy low-fat cookie is recommended for people with diabetes on special occasions.

WICKED CHOCOLATE CAKE
Makes 10 servings

Cake

¾ cup sugar

4 tablespoons light margarine (Promise®)

¾ cup boiling water

1¼ cups self-rising flour

½ teaspoon baking soda

⅓ cup cocoa powder

2 egg whites

cooking spray

Frosting

¾ cup confectioner's sugar

1 tablespoon cocoa powder

1 teaspoon light margarine (Promise®)

1-1½ tablespoons no-fat milk

To make cake: In a medium size mixing bowl completely dissolve sugar and margarine in boiling water. Sift flour, baking soda and cocoa into bowl in one go, using an electric mixer beat together for 1 minute, add egg whites and beat for 30 seconds more.

Coat a microwave round ring pan (6 cup) or a microwave dish that has a separate center piece with cooking spray. Cut out grease-proof paper to fit base of pan and line base, spray top of paper with cooking spray, coat center piece with cooking spray and place in middle.

Pour cake mix into pan and place in center of microwave (650 watt) on high for 6 minutes – 4 minutes on high for 1000 watt microwave. Leave cake in microwave for 2 minutes then remove, turn out onto a cake rack, peel off paper and leave to cool.

To make frosting: Once cake has cooled place all frosting ingredients into a small mixing bowl, add enough milk to make a spreadable consistency then spread frosting evenly over top of cake.

Variation: To make in conventional oven follow recipe but instead of using a microwave pan use a bundt pan (ringed metal cake pan) coated with cooking spray. Bake in fan-forced oven at 350°F (180°C) for approximately 30 minutes or until cake springs back in centre when touched.

Suitable to be frozen minus the frosting.

Nutritional Information

PER SERVE	FROSTING	NO FROSTING
CALORIES	183	140
TOTAL FAT	3.0g	2.8g
SATURATED FAT	0.8g	0.7g
SODIUM	210mg	204mg
CARBS	36.7g	26.2g
SUGAR	23.5g	13.2g
FIBER	0.8g	0.8g
PROTEIN	3.1g	3.0g
GI RATING	Medium	Medium

Dietitian's tip

Everyone's favourite but this cake offers little nutritional value to your diet.

Royal Easter Show 2001

1st prize

INDEX

Visit Annette's website where you will find more recipes and tips to enjoy.
Annette is a highly sort after motivational speaker and is an inspiration to all who meet her.
If you would like Annette to speak at your next function, conference or seminar then go to her website below for more details.

www.symplytoogood.com